SHORELESS BRIDGES

SOUTH EAST EUROPEAN
WRITING IN DIASPORA

STUDIES IN SLAVIC LITERATURE AND POETICS

VOLUME LV

Edited by

J.J. van Baak
R. Grübel
A.G.F. van Holk
W.G. Weststeijn

SHORELESS BRIDGES
SOUTH EAST EUROPEAN WRITING IN DIASPORA

EDITED BY
ELKA AGOSTON-NIKOLOVA

Amsterdam - New York, NY 2010

Cover design: Aart Jan Bergshoeff

The paper on which this book is printed meets the requirements of "ISO
9706:1994, Information and documentation - Paper for documents -
Requirements for permanence".

ISBN: 978-90-420-3020-6
E-Book ISBN: 978-90-420-3021-3
©Editions Rodopi B.V., Amsterdam - New York, NY 2010
Printed in the Netherlands

Table of Contents

6

Introduction: Shoreless Bridges

Elka Agoston-Nikolova

On April 18th, 2008 a group of South East European writers and scholars met at the Faculty of Arts, at the University of Groningen, the Netherlands, for a conference on *Lives in Translation. South East European Diaspora Writing Before and After 1990* with the support of the Groningen Research School for the Study of the Humanities (ICOG)[1]. They arrived from different corners of the world – Sofia, Skopje, Paris, Canterbury, Beijing, Amsterdam, The Hague – to discuss, illuminate, cast doubt, (re)define the story of exile, migration, or, on the whole, the diasporic experience.[2] Such descriptions cover only a part of the wide spectrum of writing that goes on outside the national literatures, which is multilingual, positioned between two or more languages, histories, geographies and cultures. This one-day conference was aimed at a particular mix of experience: the firsthand experience of the writers invited and the critical analyses of their work from the contributing scholars who were from both the home countries and abroad. The participants live in a number of different countries – the Netherlands, Belgium, Germany, Macedonia, Bulgaria, and the United Kingdom. Personal or political upheavals have scattered them all over Europe. Of the writers, Dubravka Ugrešić resides in Amsterdam, writing in her native Croatian, David Albahari, who was not present at the conference though his works were discussed, lives in Canada and writes in Serbian, Goran Stefanovski now lives in England and teaches and writes in English, Kica Kolbe, also not present, lives in Germany and writes in Macedonian, and Tzveta Sofronieva lives predominantly in Germany and writes in Bulgarian, German and English, and sometimes in all three at the same time. Of the scholarly contributors, Nikolaj Aretov, Penka Angelova and Dimitar Kambourov live in Bulgaria, Maja Bojadžievska and Goce Smilevski live in Macedonia, Chantal Wright lives in Canada, Ellen Elias-Bursać resides at present in The Hague, and Raymond Detrez lives in Belgium. All are engaged in acts of translation and transmission of words, images, dreams, histories (personal and collective), and cultures. These 'lives in translation' form the subject matter for the present volume, for it soon transpired during the conference that one day was not sufficient to fully explore diasporic writing, while the publication of a volume on South East European diaspora writing would open possibilities for a continuation of the discussion: is such writing just expressing a personal fate or misfortune, or is it also a mediator in the dialogue of cultures? Every one of the participants has looked at exile, emigration, or living abroad as a key experience placing them in a specific cultural space – that of the Other. All have in their particular way explored what is nowadays fashionably called a 'fluid identity', with key notions of memory, pain, estrangement, and belonging or non-belonging.

Bridges, or, most poignantly, *shoreless bridges,* was the metaphor found to encompass the heart of the discussion. First voiced by Goran Stefanovski as:

> *A process which seems not to be interested in individuals – the two banks of the river seem to be content on being banks of the river, they do not seem to need a bridge!*

It became the central image which is considered from different personal, theoretical or historical points of view in this book.

The South Slavic Diaspora before and after 1990 has seldom been the subject of scholarly studies. While the aftermath of the disembodiment of the Yugoslav Federal Republics caused a steady flow of political, historical and cultural studies, the literature written outside the South Slavic countries has not been scrutinized.

In Part I of the present volume – The Voice of the Writers – three South East European writers have written on the state of exile, literature, and the national state, and literary communication across states and languages.

Goran Stefanovski, writer, dramatist, scriptwriter, living between his native Macedonia and England, writing in Macedonian and English, voices his frustration with the state of being a 'conduit'. The process of translation often becomes so involved with itself that the original text is lost. The symbol of *Chinese Whispers* portrays here the predicament of inter-national writing, when communication becomes as unintelligible at times as "Chinese whispers" across countries, states, frontiers and other barriers. But it is the task of the writer, says Stefanovski, to "keep up the devilishly difficult balancing act"!

Tzveta Sofronieva, writer and poet, living at present in Berlin, writes in her native Bulgarian, in German, the language of her host country, and in English. Sofronieva was awarded the prestigious Adelbert von Chamisso prize in 2009, which praises part of her work, originally written in German. For the poet, however, the creative process is one uninterrupted flow. Some poems are written in all three languages. How to separate out one part – it would be like having to sever a part of her being, as though being bound to a medieval Inquisition machine and "being taken apart", forced to "splinter on the outside", but still keeping one's own identity within. For writing and poetry is a free process, which likes to play.

Poetry remains a tongue.
The tongue loves to do precisely as it sees fit.

Dubravka Ugrešić, who left Croatia in 1993 and lives at present in Amsterdam, remarks that the "fatal liaison" between literature and politics did not disappear after the fall of the Wall. Writers are seen to act either as representatives of their national literatures, or can otherwise be labeled "traitors". The recent accusations against Milan Kundera show that the "traumatic back and forth between literature and ideology is unchanged"! The terms émigré, exile, immigrant, migrant… are both discriminatory (from the home country) and affirmative, but restrictive (from the host country). Can there be an autonomous literary work when we are so entangled today in reception and market evaluation?

The Balkans as a geographical bridge and religious cross-point between the East and the West is a cliché to be found in many studies on Balkan history and culture.

The South Slavic (Balkan) oral tradition also abounds in ballads about the building of bridges or other constructions of major importance for the family or community. But no matter how strongly the foundations are built, when the builders go home for the night, the forest spirit (*vila*) destroys their work, requiring a human sacrifice. For a bridge, could only stand strong, if the young wife of the youngest master builder was to be sacrificed, immured alive into the foundations, so that her life force would secure the strength of the bridge (Vuk Karadžić, vol. 2, No. 26).

Two major Balkan novels have built a whole tapestry around the ballad of the building of a bridge. The 1961 Nobel prize winner Ivo Andrić's *Na Drini Ćuprija (The Bridge on the Drina, 1945)* tells the story of a bridge built on the River Drina at Višegrad, commissioned in 1566 by the Ottoman Grand Vizier Mehmed pasha Sokolović, in memory of the day when he and many other Slavic boys were plucked from their native villages in Bosnia, in lieu of payment of the 'devshirme' tax levied on the non-Muslim population every four years.

Ismail Kadare's *Ura Me Tri Harqe (The Three-Arched Bridge, 1978)* depicts the building of another bridge, in Albania, in 1377. Both bridges bring over foreign powers and open the Balkans to foreign occupation.

This almost banal image of the Balkans as a bridge has also shaped the identity perception of the South Slavs (Balkan peoples) as being in a transitory stage, neither here nor there:

> *Humans and Gods meet and pass each other on a bridge and on a cross-roads. In the Balkans they join in a complex process of contact – conflict, which makes them different from the ideal types of religious and ideological doctrines. In the evolution of human civilization, the Balkans are not a transitionary zone, but a space, in which humans overcome the contradictions of Gods and gods. This is a high price of life paid by numerous generations, which requires to revise the ideologemes disclosed through the metaphorical labels of the bridge and the cross-roads and the strategies resulting from them.* (quoted in *Imagining the Balkans*, Todorova, M. p.59)

Yet it is important to keep in mind that the Balkans before the formation of nation states were a patchwork quilt of multilingual and multiracial communities.

This is why Part II – Academic Discussion – starts with a case study of a 19th century South Slavic dilemma – the life and work of Grigor Parličev (1830 – 1893) who "knew most of the Balkan languages and displayed a kind of Balkanic disposition" (R. Detrez). He lived all over the Balkans, spoke and wrote in Greek, in a self-devised Common Slav language, in Bulgarian, and, when in his native town – he spoke Macedonian. His life is that of a typical emigrant and his 'case' raises one of the major questions in this volume: "Should artistic creation necessarily radiate an ethnic or national identity? Is a writer obliged to stay true to his or her native language forever?" (R. Detrez).

Nowadays an increasing number of migrants write poetry, prose, drama, non-fiction, and works of scholarship in the languages of the countries where they live. The literary paradigms of our world are changing. Yet such writing is mostly considered from the point of view of a national language and literature. Both the country of origin and the host country look upon the writer primarily as a representative of his or her native language, culture, history.

Ever since the time when Deleuze and Guattari (1986) drew attention to minority writing within a major language, with a specific reference to Yiddisch literature in Prague at the time Kafka was writing, remarking on the high degree of de-territorialisation of the language, the focus on the political aspect, and the collective value of such writing, different new disciplines have further developed these concepts, from Translation Studies to Cultural Studies and more recently Transnational Studies[3]. The proliferation of such disciplines clearly shows that there is a new category of writing which cannot be defined simply within the theoretical boundaries of existing literary theories, which have been too concerned with the national literatures and writing in one's mother tongue. We shall try here to focus on three aspects of South East European writing in the diaspora:

- What is the perception of the Self, the identity of the writer being "neither the property of a single nation nor an amorphous condition associated with postnationalism" (Apter 2006: 5)?
- What is the reception at home and in the adopted country?
- What, if any, are the theoretical and artistic characteristics of diasporic writing? What writing strategies are at the disposal of the emigrant writer?

Literature written in a non-maternal language, and, even more, bilingual writing, has often been considered lacking in knowledge of the adopted (major) language. The use of the native language in a work written in an adopted major language was seen as a sign of the inability of the writer to express himself/herself fully in the new language.

Writing in two languages, as is the case of Yoko Tawada, in whose writing, two radically different languages meet – German and Japanese, shows how "the odd juxtaposition has provided an unexpected liberation bringing with it the discovery of style filled with playfulness, humor and surrealist encounters".[4] This is how Yoko Tawada experiences the process of writing in two languages:

> I've been living in Hamburg for twenty years now. "Have you become a different person?" I am asked. "Are you a different person when you speak German?" I am asked. These questions are not easily answered. If a person were to acquire an additional personality when learning an additional language, someone who speaks five languages would possess five personalities. Should this person look like a country fair with five different booths? I don't have a single booth. I am similar to a web. The structure of a web gets denser when new traits are incorporated. In this way a new pattern is formed. There are more and more knots, tight and loose spots, irregularities, uncompleted corners, edges, holes, or superimposed layers. This web, which can catch tiny planktons, I will call a multilingual web.[5]

Such a web of superimposed layers, memories, untranslatable words applies to the poetry of Tzveta Sofronieva. Her poems, she says, are neither geographically nor linguistically determined. Her web is built of the smells of childhood, lullabies sung by mother, English, the language of freedom for her and for many East Europeans during the communist period, Russian, the language of Brodsky, one of her teachers, German, the language of her adopted country. But her poems are neither Bulgarian, or German, or English, or Canadian, or Australian, or Chinese. *They are Tzveta Sofronieva's*!

Iliya Troyanow and Dimitré Dinev, also born in Bulgaria, living outside Bulgaria, have written novels about communist Bulgaria in German, published in Germany. Their work reached Bulgaria only after it had won acclaim abroad. Nicolay Aretov's *The Gaze from Home* traces Bulgarian emigrants' writing through the 20th century until nowadays, defining the different waves of emigration from Bulgaria before and after World War II. He exposes the myths and demonization underlying the attitude towards emigrants' writing at home – propaganda, counter-propaganda, emotions, politics, all standing in the way of an objective reception. Yet the fact that it has taken quite a long period, for example, for Germany to come to terms with its past and that there was external pressure to do so (the lost war, the Nuremberg trial, etc.) should be taken into account. Most Eastern

European countries, and Bulgaria is no exception, still have to come to terms with their totalitarian heritage.

The Other Road by Penka Angelova dissects further this attitude at home, for an emigrant is expected to write "with pride of his/her Bulgaria". The author discusses how post-war Germany made sense of its painful Nazi past, cleaning the German language of false rhetoric and she speaks of the slow and painful process in post-communist Bulgaria of coming to terms with the totalitarian past. The work of Troyanov and Dinev can be seen as an appeal for a "redefinition of the past in the manipulated and hidden myth of present-day Bulgaria". Connected with the poetry and prose of Tzveta Sofronieva, these writers offer "a rapprochement of the mental worlds of a mobile world with multiple identities".

At the other end, host countries where emigrants live and work continue to look at emigrants' writing as a contribution to the national literature. The prestigious Adelbert von Chamisso Prize was awarded to Iliya Troyanow, Dimitre Dinev and Tzveta Sofronieva, as authors writing in German whose mother tongue or cultural background is not German. In *The Water under the Bridge* Chantal Wright questions the correctness of the primary aim of this literary prize – "it suggests a linguistic mold into which the Bulgarian or Argentinean or Polish tradition can be poured and which will put a presentable German face on an alien literature". It perceives thus emigrant writers, again, as bearers of their native literatures and cultures. Even more important, it seems to distract attention from the subject matter of such writing. In the case of Tzveta Sofronieva's poetry, her dialogue with American and German writers, her fascination with English literature and American culture, her consideration for male and female roles, should be taken into consideration.

Coming from the South East European region and more emphatically the Balkans introduces a political aspect to diasporic writing which seems to influence the traditional reading of emigrants' writing from these countries. Can there be literary autonomy, asks Dubravka Ugrešič?

> Even if I were to write a text about the desolation of frozen landscapes at the North Pole, I would still generally be labeled as a Croatian writer... Reviewers would promptly populate the frozen wasteland of my text with concepts such as exile, Croatia, ex-Yugoslavia, post-communism, the Balkans...

Dubravka Ugrešić and David Albahari share the trauma of the dismemberment of their country, the former Yugoslavia, into separate national states. Their refusal and personal commitment to non-nationalism has meant life in exile after both had become renowned writers in their country. In *Translating Dubravka Ugrešić and David Albahari* Ellen Elias Bursać offers an interesting analysis of their writing in exile which includes the point of view of the translator. It becomes obvious that in order to translate such work it is even more important to have been part of that world which has now disappeared. The trauma of war, of living abroad, of a lost home, the anecdote and the special brand of humor, the individual styles and themes, are conveyed by the compassionate skill of the translator.

Bulgaria – wrestling with a painful totalitarian past and a traumatic post-communist existence, Serbia and Croatia – new old nation states after a catastrophic war, Macedonia – a country caught in limbo, not even sure of its name. Each of the writers, who speak in this volume has had to experience the vicissitudes of leaving home, the struggle to remember and forget, and to forge a new identity.

A prominent dramatist in Macedonia before the war, Goran Stefanovski had to leave his home in the 1990s. Having lost his 'old story' and having not yet found a 'new one', he offers profound insights as an outsider. In "Stories from the Wild East" he exposes the falsity of national narratives: the "Western European story founded on individualism, political sterility, greed and consumerism" and "the Eastern European story based on patriarchal collectivism" (Goce Smilevski in *Goran Stefanovski – a Playwright in the Tower of Babel*).

Subverting the stereotypes, Stefanovski writes the play *Casabalkan* (1996) resurrecting the image of Casablanca in the famous 1942 film of director Michael Curtiz, as a free zone, a middle ground, a mediator between a Europe imprisoned by the Nazis and the freedom of the Americas.

The theme of Casablanca is a metaphor for Macedonia and all the small countries which lie at cross-roads. It is a synonym for an identity based on exile, non-belonging, and alienation. This theme is taken up by another Macedonian writer in exile – Kica Kolbe, a former philosophy teacher at the University of Skopje, a child of ethnic Macedonians who were driven from their homes in Northern Greece. Maja Bojadžievska in *Fragments between Desire and*

Nostalgia: A Macedonian Case discusses Kica Kolbe's life and work as a challenge to the narrative of belonging to a particular form of identity. She was caught in the problematic vision of 'home', first of her parents as refugees and then of her second migration – this time from ex-Yugoslavia. As a refugee, Dina, Kica Kolbe's protagonist in *Snow in Casablanca,* is representative of the diasporic culture of the Balkans. "She moves easily along the luminal spaces of identity and all she does is, in fact, translation". When Dina returns to Skopje, the first sensation which strikes her consciousness is the scent, the perfume of that 'something' which is conventionally called home.

It is also through "the scent of mama" that Tzveta Sofronieva in her poem *Ein Unbekantes Wort* (*An Unknown Word*) defines her identity in terms of belonging:

> Der Ort des Bewohnens kann Berlin sein,
> Beverly Hills, Bitterfeld, Konska, Paris.
> Hauptsache es richt nach Mama.

The topos of memory, as all the essays in this volume note, is central to diasporic literature, for "memory is a phenomenon of conceptual border zones".[6] According to Dimitar Kambourov in *Exile or Exodus: D. Ugrešić's The Museum of Unconditional Survival and Iliya Troyanow's The World is Big and Salvation Lurks around the Corner*, it is made of "a rare recipe, mixing reminiscences, myopia, boredom, irony and pain". Whether it is the mechanism of Proust's *memoire involuntaire,* or fragments of Bulgarian lullaby song, or the random museum, the photo album, the hobby collection, or memories of the protagonists 'mother' and 'father' – these are all "anchors in an otherwise unanchored, displaced existence" (Ellen Elias Bursać). It is through the power of fiction and poetry that space is organized as a multiplicity of spaces, "a symbolic act which makes space look like time – i.e. unidirectional and fluid" (Kambourov).

Such writing can be seen as a bridge, bringing worlds and cultures face-to-face. This hides in itself a silent double image, a hidden image of tension between two worlds", as it is most daringly pictured in one of Frank Kafka's shortest stories, *The Bridge*" (Maja Bojadžievska). Kafka's image of the human bridge stretched painfully between the two shores, epitomizes the question raised at the beginning of this book: Can a diasporic writer be a bridge between two or more languages and cultures? And if so, how can one accomplish such "a balancing act"? Is there a third possibility, asks Goce Smilevski in his article on Goran Stefanovski – neither cruel collectivism, nor escapism? Or is it too late for that question, as the choice has been made… " Is it possible, asks Dubravka Ugrešić, to step out of "the hellish circle, where the autonomy of a literary text is only another name for politicization, and politicization another name for autonomy"? And what about all the new developments which enforce dramatic changes in writing and reading – the younger generation's language of text messages, mass media culture, the powerful global Internet zone, e-books, etc.?

If, we (diasporic, exophone) writers create bridges, writes Tzveta Sofronieva, it could be a coincidence, an inspiration, but this is never static. Such literature strives to "achieve balance between order and disorder, between a meaninglessly bare life and its meaningful interpretation" (Kambourov).

When the old narratives are no longer meaningful, can these bridge-texts introduce a new methodology of diasporic writing with ideas of open literary spaces, multilingual webs, alternative narratives (where the narrator plays the role of mediator between reader and experience), new definitions of the concepts of home and abroad…?

Created in times of crisis and change, suffering alternately from amnesia and too much remembering, and precariously positioned at a cross-roads of different spaces, histories and languages, South East European diasporic writing "opens up for a nomadic attitude based on indifferent indiscriminate love for the world structured as a journey rather than a home, as time rather than as place" (Kambourov). It offers a critical approach, an alternative model of writing in a world of continuous change.

Notes
[1] The program of the conference can be consulted at the site of ICOG:
   www.rug.nl/let/onderzoekinstituten/ICOG/archief/events2008.
[2] There are a multitude of terms used nowadays: exiles, emigrants, migrants, refugees, or the 'intellectual nomads' of Edward Said. They are, says Dubravka Ugrešić in her essay, both "discriminatory and also affirmative". For lack of more precise word we shall limit ourselves here to: 'diasporic writing', 'exilic literature' and 'exophone writers'.
[3] See Emily Apter *The Translation Zone* and Azade Seyhan *Writing Outside the Nation.*
[4] *Lives in Translation*, ed. Isabelle de Courtivron, N.Y., Palgrave Macmillan, 2003, p.2

[5] Ibid. p.148
[6] Azade Seyhan, Writing Outside the Nation, p.31

Bibliography

Andrić, Ivo. 1966 (1945). *Na Drini Ćuprija* (*The Bridge over the Drina*), Sarajevo: Svjetost.

Apter, Emily. 2006. *The Translation Zone.* Princeton and Oxford: Princeton University Press.

Azade, Seyhan. 2001. *Writing Outside the Nation.* Princeton and Oxford: Princeton University Press.

Courtivron de, Isabelle. 2003. *Lives in Translation.* New York: Palgrave Macmillan.

Deleuze, Gilles and Felix Guattari. 1986. *Kafka. Towards a Minor Literature.* Minneapolis London: University of Minnesota Press.

Kadare, Ismail. 1997. *The Three-Arched Bridge* (*Ura Me Tri Harge*, 1978) (tr. John Hodgson). New York: Arcade Publishing.

Karadžić, V. St. *Srpske narodne pjesme* ("Zidanje Skadra" vol. 2, No. 26) in *Sabrana dela Vuka Karadžića.* vols. 1–4. Belgrade: Prosveta 1975 ff.

Todorova, Maria. 1997. *Imagining the Balkans.* New York Oxford: Oxford University Press.

Part I

The Voice of the Writers

Chinese Whispers

Goran Stefanovski

I was kindly invited to this Conference (*"Lives in Translation"*) as a practicing playwright.

Making my way here, I met someone on the train from Canterbury East to London Victoria. He is a small, slightly pompous man with a waxed moustache. He used to write for hi-fi magazines, but he says he now writes about watches. Writes about watches? I was curious, but I asked no questions.

He asked me where I was going. I gave him the program for this Conference. He glanced at it and was immediately dismissive. "Another EU scam" he said, in a Mister-know-it-all way. This was a very British attitude to a very European initiative. I already felt silly. He asked me what my mandate was. I asked him what he meant by that. He said: "Who do you represent, what permission do you have, who's the muscle behind you, what's the authority?" I said I represented myself. He said "Why do they want you there?" I said "Some friends invited me to speak." "Why you," he said. "Because they like me," I answered glibly. "Oh come on," he said, "it's never about that, it's always about something else." "What?" I asked. "You should ask yourself that question" he said. "You are not a mascot are you? You are not a token?" This hurt.

So I've been asking myself that question. Had I come here on academic business, as a lecturer and representative of my Department of Media, I would have been legitimate. But this time that's not the case. So indeed who do I represent? It's both a simple and a metaphysical question.

Who do I represent when I get commissioned by producers to write a play? Do I represent them or myself? Or my audience? What happens when I just write a piece, when I commission it myself? Whose mandate is it then? My super ego? My Id? I suppose it's all of these, in constant negotiation. Did Shakespeare have a mandate from the Globe Theatre Ltd. to write another play? Did Bach have a mandate from his church in Cothen to write another Christmas oratorio?

So here I am, talking about living and writing between two languages and having to talk about it today. I find this an important task. I am very eager about it, even starry-eyed. I like to be an interface. A conduit. To give and take. To interchange. To engage in transmission, interpretation, translation. But who do I translate for? If you are one bank of the river, and I am the bridge, who and what is my other bank? Who am I a middle ground, channel, confluence and catalyst for? Who do I link and connect?

When I was a child in elementary school I was also eager and starry-eyed. One day I was elected president of the class. The teacher congratulated me, as did some of my peers. I was excited. Then I realized I didn't understand what that meant. I wanted to be active and useful, but what was there to do? The pupils didn't care about my title, the teachers didn't either. It seemed to be an honorary title, ceremonial, ritualistic, totemic. It turned out I was inefficient middle ground. A frustrated conduit.

There was one major power which was bestowed on me, however. On certain Monday mornings the teachers would check how clean our hands were. So, prior to this, I had the power to ask everyone to show me their fingernails. It was the power of a hygienist. Most of the 'clean' pupils would show me their fingernails without even being asked. And the thugs, who I knew were dirty, I didn't dare ask as I knew they would beat me up. So I hung on to my empty title. At least my parents were proud of it.

These kinds of ceremonial titles seem to have followed me through life. I went on being eager and starry-eyed and president in high school and university too. Then I went on being eager and starry-eyed and I wrote a few plays. And they made me member of juries and invited me to conferences. As a representative of who and what? I was never quite sure. But I always hoped to be active and useful and interfacing.

Then I met my English wife and believed I was representing Macedonia in England and England in Macedonia. Then I was elected a member of the Macedonian Academy of Arts and Sciences. And recently I was given the honorary title of Cultural Ambassador of the Republic of Macedonia to the United Kingdom. This is who you are dealing with here.

What I'm really complaining about is that I never get paid for these positions. If I did, I wouldn't mind feeling useless from time to time. The novelist Dubravka Ugrešić told me that is how she felt when she was invited to the Frankfurt International Book Fair. She found herself surrounded with too many publishers and soon realized that the whole affair was about them and not about her. It made her feel like a mascot, a token.

But trying to interface is never easy. It gets pretty ugly when we fail to interface, when our representation goes haywire.

When I lived in my native Republic of Macedonia I would write a play, the theatre would put it on and that was pretty much it and that was enough. But the times changed. A European producer comes to town and says I want to work with you as a representative of Macedonia. I am eager and starry-eyed and I want to interface. I go with him to Europe. I hope to be a middle ground, a confluence, a catalyst, a conduit.

At that moment a few doors shut behind me in my home country. Voices are raised. He is working for them now! He is a not our proper representative any more. "But I do represent us," I say. They say "No, once you represent us to them, you don't represent us anymore." "So who should I represent us to, then?" "No one. No one is worthy of our representation." "And who should do this representation to no one?" "Only the genuine representatives, who know how to properly not represent us." "I don't get it," I say. "You see. You now don't even understand these basic truths. We take the mandate from you." So there you go. That's how you lose one mandate you don't understand and get another you understand even less.

Over the years I've met people who leave their families, languages, states, nations, theatres and audiences and travel far and wide, eager and starry-eyed, hoping to translate, to bridge, to link. And often getting lost. The process seems not to be interested in them, being bent on itself. The two banks of the river are content being self-contained and don't seem to need a bridge. Or if there is an attempt at translation it gets precious and involved with itself. The original text is lost. The intended reader is abandoned. The conduit becomes a barrier.

I worked with a little theatre company in the UK. They would spend months on paperwork, filling in Inter-reg. forms, Arts Council applications, progress reports. They would even hire someone to write them for them. After endless audience-building workshops there was little time and energy left for theatre as I knew it. The channels and drains were blocked and overflowing.

I grew up in the sixties. People shat, pissed, threw up, farted and copulated on stage. One of the most unforgettable experiences I've seen in the theatre was a piece performed by the London-based, nomadic and accidental, performance group called the People's Show. I saw them at a theatre Festival in Sarajevo, last century, in 1972. They were starry-eyed and eager and reckless and wild.

The little studio stage had a backdrop of some rusty metal stuff they had found that morning in a junk yard. On the stage there was Jeff Nuttal, a leonine figure wearing an apron, with a broom in his hands. Centre stage was an immobile young man sitting at a table, wearing a sharp and pristine striped suit and black glasses. On the table in front of him was a loaf of bread, ketchup, eggs, cream cheese, a carton of milk and a huge butcher's knife.

Very slowly and methodically the man started making a sandwich. Then he buried the knife in the carton so that the milk spurted out and went all over the table and all over his expensive suit. Whatever went on the floor, the man with the broom swept towards the audience, which retreated to the back, giggling hysterically.The young man went on squeezing the cheese and ketchup on the loaf, breaking the eggs, making a terrible mess. In the end he buried his face in this sandwich-from-hell. Pure immediate theatre! It had a therapeutic effect on me. I've tried all of my life not to spill milk on my clothes. I promised myself that one day I would put on my Sunday best and eat like the Dadaist pig I once saw on that stage. I still haven't acted upon that promise.

Last year, by chance, I stumbled upon the People Show theatre in Bethnal Green. They now have a building all of their own! I wondered how much they now have to worry about the Borough regulations, the Arts Council, political correctness, aims and targets, equal opportunities, cultural diversity, annual reports. Has the wild source been bottled up? Has the force become an institution, the process a place? Has the underground become overground, has the radical fringe become accepted mainstream? Have they become a mascot, a token for the culture of underprivileged East London?

In Byzantium the bureaucracy turned the state into its own service. Today's government ministries are often so busy dealing with their own problems that they forget the public. Academics find students a nuisance; doctors would work so much better if only there were not all these patients. Some days my computer gets so bogged down with its internal sophisticated software processes that I can't use it even as a simple type writer.

A museum in Macedonia is better kept shut in winter, because if it opened its doors to the public it would have to spend all its meager funds on heating and risk being shut down completely. So in order to survive and stay open it has to be closed to the public. And so we arrive at the farcical status quo, the Byzantine stasis. The conduit has become a buffer, a barrier, a limbo, no man's land, quarantine, a decompression chamber which keeps things compressed.

They say you can measure poetry by what is lost in its translation. How much meaning is lost in translation? How much energy is lost in transmission? How much art is lost in the management of art? How much communication is lost in Chinese whispers? (Or conversely, in an ideal world, how much might be even gained in these processes.)

We are all in the business of interfacing. I have come here to praise the importance of our job, but to also remind us of the devilishly difficult balancing act that goes with it. We must get it right so that we don't end up like the defunct, no-more-bridging, ex-London Bridge in the desert of Arizona.

The moral of the story: keep your interface active and creative and alive and kicking!

Un-lost in Translation

Tzveta Sofronieva

Am I one of these people

Standing on Ellis Island as a Bulgarian tourist at the beginning of the final decade of the twentieth century, I bought a yellowish-looking postcard showing an old photograph of arrivals in the U.S. and sent it to my German fiancé; at that time I spoke English with him since my German was none-existent, as was his Bulgarian. While trying to express my feelings – of a traveler between the worlds at the end of a Communist era, standing on Ellis Island having just visited the Statue of Liberty, I wrote a poem instead. The poem, *Am I one of these people*, was, as were my thoughts at that moment, about the English language; it was written in English, and the stamped postcard flew to Berlin:

> A traveller, I wander between
> suitcases and somewhere to belong
> […]
> I am a soul whose music is a mix
> of confused sounds, new, unpredictable,
> drunk, tired, murmuring, grumbling,
> loving, falling, loving, traveling sounds […].

Later on I wrote this poem in (or you might prefer to say – translated it into) Bulgarian and it was published in my second book of poetry *Зачеваща памет* (*Conceiving memory*) in 1995. I translated it from the English original into German and in 1996 it was discussed with fellow poets at the *Akademie Schloss Solitude* before a reading in Stuttgart, and then, later on, edited further (or you might prefer to say – translated from the Bulgarian version) by Gabi Tiemann, in the course of a long conversation we had, and was subsequently published in German in my collection *Gefangen im Licht* (*Caught in the Light*) in 1999. It first appeared in English in a slightly altered version in *Transcript* (www.transcript-review.org) in 2007 – the alterations were the result of rewriting the poem in different languages and working on it in California in 2005. So the original of this poem from 1992 was either never published or it was published as several clones many times. Which of these claims is true?

On the last day of 1990, sitting in the guest room of the library at the *Deutsches Museum* where I was a visiting fellow in December 1990, I found myself in real trouble since I was invited to spend New Year's Eve with dear friends of mine but I had no present for them and had no money for flowers or anything else. On the table near me there was an old typewriter, I suppose for decoration, as a historical artifact, since everyone I knew there used a computer already. And since the typewriter was the only tool I had and words were the only free material available, I took a piece of paper and placed it in the machine so that I could type along its widest edge and began typing my present:

Sometimes

the wine is white and red and pink and purple if you love it
the streets are munich montreal paris and mars the moon you love
the men are black and white and green and blue which you may love
women are blonde with colored eyes and brown lips for you to love
the year is gorbachev or bush or hussein or me or me and you who love
the day is first and last and work and fun and past and present future
days of love which could be yellow orange light or dark as you do love [...].

It was a poem in English, since my friends and I spoke English with one another. They were both medical scientists who spoke fluent English, one of them was American, and I didn't speak any German at the time. Joseph Brodsky was later to read and enjoy this poem. The poem was published in Bulgarian and in English in 1992 in my book *Chicago Blues*, a book written both in Bulgarian and English, as a diary on the road, as a present to all the people I met on the road, as an investigation on the road and of the road.

Journey to the West

The poem *Journey to the West* was written both in Bulgarian and in English, and thought in both languages, since it was lived through in English when I spent time in Canada in 1989 and was about my feelings of friendship for Margaret Atwood and her wonderful book on Susanna Moodie, on immigration, on Canada, on women, on starting all over again. It was published in both langauges in *Chicago Blues* and I made a German version of the poem for the presentation of the poetry collection in Berlin in August 1992. Today everyone reads this poem as though I had written it about my exophonic existence in the German language.

> A word in an unknown language.
> I know there must be a sense,
> must be a meaning.
> It's probably marginal.
> Maybe a preposition
> or a noun.
> Either used often or
> too strange for the ear.
> Learning all languages
> I listen attentively
> to the springs of their speech.
> I follow the air in the circles
> of the vowels coming to me
> from mouths of people
> close to me and far away;
> search for a language in which
> I am a word.

At the beginning of May 2003, following a reading and a discussion on the expansion of the EU in the *Literaturhaus Stuttgart*, I wrote the poem *Für Europa werben* (*Endorsing Europe*) in German on one of those paper napkins you find on restaurant tables, and this original remained with one of my colleagues from the discussion. Later on that summer, in Bulgaria, feeling how excited people there were about the possibility of joining the EU, I wrote the poem again, in Bulgarian, and this Bulgarian version met with great interest because of the then current movement towards EU accession. A translator and a friend translated it into German after it had been published in Bulgarian in the *Lirika* year book and I told her that in German I had thought this or that line differently and it was edited accordingly. Then the poem appeared in a German academic journal dedicated to the Slavic languages, as a translation. However, the original (or shall I say one of the originals?) of this poem was German, written on a particular day in a particular space under particular circumstances. And when I was preparing my recent collection of *Deutsche Gedichte* (*German Poems*) (2008), the editor and I thought that this poem should not be omitted from a book that was very much about identity. Of course, my translators into German have translated many of my poems that were originally written in Bulgarian without my intervention, in purely their own versions, and I like these and I am very grateful to my translators. It is the exceptions, however, that are much more interesting when discussing exophonic work and its relationship to translation.

In German, which I have studied since I was almost thirty years old, I initally felt as though I was lacking an awareness of how my poetry worked. In the beginning I needed to re-write a poem written in German in Bulgarian, in order to feel what this poem was doing. And Bulgarian is certainly not a language in which I would like to read translations of my poems. When the poem *Sometimes*, which I wrote in English, was published in Bulgarian in the journal *Poljanitza* in a strange version by someone without any copyright permission, even though I had already written and published this poem in Bulgarian, I realized that my originals cannot be only in one language no matter how the external world looks at this. I can never ever consider my Bulgarian (versions of my) poems as translations, no matter how the poems were first written, since I write them in Bulgarian after erasing them in any other language. In contrast, there are poems which I could never think in Bulgarian.

It is certainly very uncool to tell these stories. It would be better to construct fashionable, success-inducing narratives. Stories which sell.

Poetry remains a tongue

Both in Germany and in Bulgaria my publishers preferred not to mention that the collections included some poems with twins as originals or with my own versions in two or three languages. The German editor of my book *Eine Hand voll Wasser* (*A Hand Full of Water*), insisted on the special subtitle "Deutsche Gedichte" (German

Poems) and the same thing happened with the book *Drei Frauen* (Three Women), which contained 'purely Bulgarian poems' that a German colleague who does not speak Bulgarian was supposed to *nachdichten* (*re-versify*) on the basis of interlinear translations and my own remarks. I remembered Brodsky and Kundera who developed such strong feelings about how their work sounded in other languages that they themselves began either to translate it or to work directly in English and French respectively. Brodsky often reworked translations of his Russian poems into English, made by others, in order, in his own words, "to bring them closer to the original", and I like his versions very much. It seems to me that when that moment comes when you feel you know what you are doing in a second language and one version of a poem is for you the only right one and you cannot easily accept another, then that language has already become your exophonic literary language.

It was bizarre for me to live through the strange process of being forced to separate from a part of myself and to look at it as if it were not me and then to switch these parts as if I were a machine offering different programs at the touch of a button. I felt as though I were bound to a medieval inquisition wheel, where I was being taken apart and whatever I said was understood only as an additional statement of guilt. I was forced to splinter on the outside and keep my integrity only within. We cannot include your entire bibliography, said the organization that awards the *Adelbert-von-Chamisso-Preis*, we only need what was originally written in German. As if there were no me before this, as if it did not matter to my poems in German that I was a poet before them. To me, they are all my poems. They are not Bulgarian, not German, not English, not Canadian, not Australian and not Chinese. They are

> more german than the germans
> more chinese than the chinese
> more american than the americans
> more bulgarian than the bulgarians
> and so on
> I like to push nonsense into the grotesque [...]
> (from *Attaining Citizenship on Valentine's Day*, 2005, translated from German by C. Wright).

They are Tzveta Sofronieva's. They are neither geographically nor linguistically determined. Still, I am constantly being asked to force my poems into a frame, into a box. For me

> Poetry remains a tongue.
> The tongue loves to do precisely as it sees fit. (from *Merci, Paris*, 2005, ibid.)

And I feel as though putting poetry in a box is an abuse of poetry. Since poetry needs to erase language and create it anew.

Today we talk a lot about multiculturalism but it is dichotomies that continue to sell best and the space between them is considered most difficult for a writer. I do not define my place as a space between dichotomies, however, and in my space there is no need for them and no need to make a choice between them. In the space I inhabit one does not live with the notion of dichotomies, one does not think this way at all.

Between

> the permitted dream
> and a piece of the dream I always dreamed.
>   Between.
> Choice is somewhere else.
> Somewhere where there's no choice.
> No choice exists
> in a room called "Between". (from *Between*, 1992, original in English)

For a long time I felt as though I were a different person in the different languages, thought that these languages were like parallel universes between which I jumped, moved and balanced. Today I know that it was not the languages that made me different but rather it was I who needed to learn to trust my own universe. Bulgarian holds all the smells from my childhood and they are always there. It is as if a woman has separated from a beloved man and meets him thousands of years later but still recognizes him by the scent of his skin. I have studied English since I was four years old. For the longest time I equated English with freedom. It is a language which tells me that you are allowed to be as you are, you do not need to satisfy the interests of others, the expectations of others. I came to Canada at a time when there was Communism in Bulgaria and entered the U.S. on foot at

Niagara Falls on a sunny day when the border guard looking at my Bulgarian passport smiled brightly and said: "Welcome to America". It is not easy to forget this feeling even though I realize how naive it is. It was also the first time I was away from the patriarchal society of the Balkans – a border to Islam – for a longer period and I felt free emotionally, was curious about new ideas and lifestyles. English was a liberation. Bulgarian with its smells and English with its freedom have remained in all the other languages in which I speak or write. Russian was the language I learned and spoke with my friends in the neighborhood as a child; it carries the taste of bonbons and diminutives in all other tongues. Serbian was the language closest to the dialect my grandfather spoke in Western Bulgaria and it reminds me of old stories and historical narratives. French was the tongue of deceit, and so on, and so on. German demands that I express myself playfully and deliberately all at the same time, that thoughts are completed before I write them, that the beginning is never forgotten when the end is reached, the grammar is almost overly precise. German for me was investigating and seeking and finding, it was like learning to walk again.

All languages are present in a new language. But are they really there? Is this all not just nonsense? I think that it is only ourselves who are present, the way we were when we were intimately involved with these languages. It is only ourselves, extracting what we need from these languages. We only ever learn what we need. Everything else gets forgotten. The same is true for words.

Unknown word

Unknown word, a poem about nostalgia, which ends with the lines

> I have never thought of
> looked for
> needed words of acknowledgement or belonging

was written in California in June of 2005. It was written in German, English and Bulgarian all at once; it was written 'mixed'; it was felt and thought and written as a flow of songs in all these languages and about the necessity or non-necessity of translating. It was written for my daughter who moves between these languages and mixes them as children often do, since children want both to be precise and to make it easy for themselves. It was written for my grandfather who used to change the old folk songs to suit his life. It was written for all those people who do not believe in homesickness. What happened to this poem? Is this poem's original in German? In English? In Bulgarian? How should I define the original and differentiate it from a translation? What is a translation in this case?

The advice was always to claim one version of a poem as an original. I am not that type of person though. I am not eager to confirm the stories of others in order to be more marketable. I did not leave Communism and Bulgaria in order to create new lies and to tell new fairytales. This has nothing to do with investigation, with aesthetics, with creativity and with communication. I am not sure I am someone or something that can be put in one frame. And this, in my view, is true for many others, too. This is why I am discussing it.

After the realization that no political power, no particular culture, no nation, no race, no sex, no way of life can impose itself on others, we arrived at the view that everything has the right to mutually exist and that nothing is translatable or comparable. This, however, led to a situation that was not much better, since the only way of succeeding in keeping a peaceful balance after recognizing the difficulty and even impossibility of mutual understanding, is to try over and over again to communicate. Dichotomies help in the analysis of complicated issues only sometimes and can be used only if one bears in mind that the pragmatic choice of a method should find its boundaries. Maybe I am overly burdened by my education in physics, but I always remember that if I want to assess the time it will take me to get from Berlin to

Frankfurt by car, then I will use the formula of the velocity of the car and the distance in kilometers in order to find the approximate time I will need for travel. I and the car will be simple particles moving from A to B. No light will be taken into account. However, if I think about movement, I had better not ignore the Theory of Relativity. Similarly, when I think about gender issues, I do better to step away from ready-made feminism, and to think instead about the right of existence of different points of view. Dichotomies developed in patriarchal societies were in fact replaced by those developed in liberal societies. When I came to Germany it was fine to be a mother and stay home taking care of one's beautiful baby and it was fine to be a professional woman who goes out to work. For both paths there was a plurality and no matter whether homosexual or heterosexual, with or without a partner, in a traditional family or in another structure, with an own or an adopted child, unwillingly childless or dedicated to the job and not wanting children, all was possible within the framework: mother or career woman. For me this dichotomy was no different than the one offered by patriarchal societies because it robbed me of choice.

Views constructed around opposing poles or shores certainly do not function for me, perhaps for none of us. They work with static notions and belong to the grand old narratives of the history of culture – narratives like national and world literatures, Central European and Balkan, the nature and absence of genre, monolingualism and multilingualism, major and minor languages, traditional and modern, stimulus and response etc. These are of little help when examining literature today, and in particular when examining diaspora and/or exophonic and/or multilingual literature. Diaspora writing should rather be examined as a variety of literary, linguistic and individual choices, and exophonic literature seen as an expression of hybrid, multi-layered, transformative literary spaces.

If you want to cross: go ahead, swim, fly

The bridge is the metaphor with which one is confronted most often when one lives a mobile and multilingual life. The moment one gets rid of the opposing shores, of the dichotomies, which require bridges by definition, a space opens up, allowing a new way of looking at things or at least an attempt at moving in this direction. It is a common situation nowadays for a person to leave his or her native place. No-one considers this a big deal or a topic worthy of long discussion. The moment one changes language in the process of changing places, however, this is considered immigration. One can move from Munich to Berlin and it is fine, but if one moves from Görlitz to the Polish town just across the bridge over the Oder, this is considered a huge step, although it does not involve any distance at all. I have never been able to understand this and have never been willing to accept it. I am a tenant, a traveler and I deeply believe that this is what we all are. Where and how we land is the result of coincidence – where you are born, where your parents find work, where the nearest school is, where the cheapest rent is or the shortest commute, where you can earn a living, where you are most seduced by your own curiosity about a place, the person with whom you fall in love, whether a war about oil is raging, whether the weather is –20 or +20 Celsius, and so on. We can of course choose directions, we are not toys in the hands of some goddess of fortune, and our decisions are very important. However, the range of situations or strategies we choose from is coincidental. It is the interplay between our decisions and the self-organization of matter that counts. In these processes a person can live everywhere and still use his or her first language privately and literarily, even if their family is forced or has chosen to adopt a new language on the outside, in their professional or social lives. Therefore, why someone leaves a language and chooses a new one seems to me a much more important issue than the fact of the currently common situation of changing places.

Exophony is certainly a more interesting topic than physical migration in terms of its decision *for* the Other, for its investigation of oneself and the world with and through that which is different, alien, unpredictable. This decision has nothing or at least has very little to do with countries, nations, geographies, and hence also not with metaphors such as that of the bridge; it is a decision to think *in* new structures and not *about* new structures or connections between them, and this, to me, makes a huge difference.

As a child I studied other languages because I wanted to communicate with people from other parts of the world, to have a chance to meet them – in the world I grew up in, it was a miracle when this opportunity came and I wanted to use it and *really* know what was going on in other places. I did not trust mediators much.

Maybe because the whole history of the Balkans was suffused by numerous foreign dominations and many mediators.

Drink straight from the source, I always remind myself. The title of the poem which includes these lines, *A Hand full of Water*, became the titel of a whole poetry collection in 2008. Abolishing mediators requires courage and strength, the courage to interpret yourself and the will to understand, to ask questions of others and to question yourself.

However, why does one – why did I – change language as an adult when outside circumstances did not dictate it? Why does one lose time in a period of one's life that is strongly geared towards achievement rather than towards re-orienting oneself? If there are excellent translators available, why does one write a novel in one's fifth language, rather than in one's first (Bulgarian) where the publishing industry would respond immediately, or in one's second (English) which is spoken by many more readers and where the book market is much larger. Does one look for a challenge simply because one loves a challenge? Is man a *Homo ludens*? This much I know in any case, and I believe I am not the only person to whom it applies: one does not choose a new language in order to become a bridge.

The idea of the bridge is imposed on the writer later on, from the outside. In one's new, adopted environment, one is confronted with the fact that one comes from a different context and a different language. One is constantly asked questions about one's origins even if only the slightest hint of an accent exists, not to mention if one has a very different way of looking at things or if one's physical appearance is very different. In Sofia I do not feel much different than I do in Vienna: it is one of the places in the world where I understand the language well. It is a *without* whose language I speak very well. One's *within* is the place you pedominatly live at the moment, where you currently rent an apartment, pay electricity bills, buy bread, send your child to school, enjoy the weather and any number of other everyday things. However, the more interesting *within* is the inner world that I take with me everywhere and inhabit and investigate.

Curriculum Vitae

Faced with writing a CV, I cannot give much data. And I feel that most interpretations of my biography are simply wrong. To say that I have a PhD from the Bulgarian Academy of Sciences is true and also false because all my research was done under the supervision of American and English and Israeli and Canadian professors in North American universities. To say that I left Bulgaria for political reasons in the late 80s is true and also false for I have always come for political reasons *back* to Bulgaria too and because today I would certainly *also* leave Bulgaria for political reasons. To say that my poetry skills were honed by Joseph Brodsky is true and false because I did study with him but no more intensively than with many poets from Bulgaria and other countries, both in person and through the study of literature. Seferis had a greater impact on me in my high school years than Cavafy, even though I adore Cavafy not less than Brodsky did. Szymborska interested me more then Milos, Rilke's prose was as important for me as Rilke's poetry, Celan and Canetti more than Goethe und Thomas Mann. Brodsky and I conversed. Although he appeared to be a resolute thinker and poet, he was open and deeply understanding and appreciating. The West often underestimates what an assertive claim means in the Eastern European tradition: a claim and a certain point of view is often a provocation, the start of a Platonic dialogue. Brodsky certainly conversed this way and through him I was encouraged to pursue this manner of writing, to stay true to the point where poetry begins. From Brodsky I also took the absolute certainty that the migrant's fate is not the exclusive property of artists and writers; that sound and thought, content and form are always together in a poem and in life. There was, however, not one mention of diaspora writers as bridges. Bridges belong to cities like Venice, Istanbul, Paris, those cities

> built on a river, are full of bridges
> and are more beautiful and more fragile than all other cities (from *Merci, Paris*,
> 2005, translated from German by C. Wright).

and in these cities bridges often connect historical eras rather then geographical shores.

My own experiences from a poet's life in translation and from building exophonic and intercultural networks makes me smile at words such as immigrant, migrant, exile, biography and other terms connected with geography, with renting places. Since I believe that we all actually only rent a bit of time in order to create a space. When we create a space it might, by coincidence, occasionally be a bridge space. However, the bridge is most often a sculpture, an inspiration for others and for oneself to continue to (learn to) fly, swim, ski, climb, pass through and so on, in order to surmount the crevice. It is only in this metamorphosed bridge, as in the epilogue of the *Correspondence with Kappus* cycle (2008, translated from German by C. Wright), that one might find a metaphor for the diasporic writer.

> [A] bridge, raised up, juts out at one shore
> outstretched, graceful, tall
> no longer a bridge
> if you want to cross: go ahead, swim, fly,
>
> swimming times, flying time
>
> beauty.

And even this is not created by him/her but rather by others. An exophonic author would be the last person to define him-/ herself in static terms.

I would rather formulate my CV, here translated from Bulgarian, in the following manner:

> I traveled, saw, met people,
> heard love, voices,
> knew beauty and freedom,
> after me ran myths I do not remember.

If I was looking for a metaphor for my own writing, I would, at the moment, use that of skiing or flying. Skis and wings are not dichotomies, they are two fully equal tools necessary both to execute and to understand a movement.

> If you can shift your weight
> then you master the moments.
> Everything about the movement depends upon
> a person finding favour in their direction.
>
> (*The Old Man, the Valley, Perhaps a Woman*, 2009, translated from German by C. Wright)

Skiing, swimming, flying etc. suggest metaphors where space and time are intertwined rather than geographical metaphors. Through them we think about ways of moving, about the impetus to begin something, about directions and how they change.

Telemachus's Dream

Dubravka Ugrešić

The Wall has fallen. It has fallen on everyone, on all of us, a friend of mine once said, with a tinge of melancholy in his voice.

True, it has fallen on all of us. It has fallen on Telemachus, too.

I spent 1994 in Berlin. This was Berlin only five years after the Wall came down. I experienced it less as a city, more as a metaphor reflecting the Yugoslav tragedy. I came across a Greek fellow, Telemachus, in Berlin, a drunkard, who played the baglamas in restaurants and lived off the coins that were tossed in his cap.

At *Terzo Mondo* Inn, Telemachus explained to me excitedly that the world is a whole and that all things in this world are connected. For instance, in November 1989, Telemachus had an unusual dream: he saw two crossed axes and himself, Telemachus, sharpening them.

"The object itself, I mean the axe, is not unfamiliar to me. In my younger days I used to earn my living chopping wood for people", said Telemachus.

The next day, the Berlin Wall collapsed. To begin with Telemachus thought that his dream had made the Berlin Wall fall. But then he discovered that his dream was about something else, about building another wall.

"I'm afraid it was I who provoked the war in your country", he said to me.

The war in Yugoslavia was still on in 1994, and Telemachus had been trying for several years already to summon that dream of his again and separate the axes.

Today, fifteen years later, I have learned that history is, indeed, written by the victors, but also that a parallel history exists. In other words: it is equally possible that the Wall fell thanks to Telemachus, as that it fell thanks to Gorbachev as he himself likes to claim. I must add here, that at a time of 'ideological depolitization', at a time when war criminals at the Hague Tribunal still stubbornly declare themselves innocent of the crimes committed, and when Serbs, Croats and others continue to insist on their criminals as heroes, Telemachus, the drunkard and baglamas player, assumes for me the stature of a moral hero. He is the only one I know who feels guilt for what he'd unconsciously done, and is ready to repair the damage.

However, I am not going to talk about the fall of the Wall, but rather about less visible and less important consequences of its fall, about literature and art. Let me start with a distant reference, Upton Sinclair, author of the novel *Oil!* Sinclair would have stayed half-forgotten as a classic of American literature had there not been a film adaptation of the novel, called *There Will Be Blood*, which blew the dust off of Sinclair's name for a moment.

Having seen the movie, I thought back to the shelf of books in my mother's apartment and the book cover of the first Yugoslav edition of *Oil!*, entitled *Petrolej*. There were pencil drawings all over the inside: these, my mother said, were my first childish scribblings. It was a post-war time, just after World War II, a time of poverty, and the covers of books doubled as drawing pads. Upton Sinclair's novel *Oil!*, Maxim Gorky's *The Mother*, and Theodore Dreiser's *American Tragedy* were some of the first titles in the home library of my young parents.

I don't remember whether I ever actually read *Oil!*. Probably not, but if I did, back when I was a student – earnestly dedicated to comparative literature – I wouldn't have dared say so out loud. At that time, defense of the 'autonomy of the literary text' (of any work of art) was something nearly sacred to every student of comparative literature, and I certainly perceived myself as battling on the front lines. In my student days 'literary autonomy' was closely tied to literary taste. In simple terms, we felt that good writers did not embark on politics – or write about life in overly real terms. Real life was left to bad writers and those who flirted with politics. The fashion of the day was the 'literariness' of literature.

Yugoslav writers were never seriously infected with the virus of socialist realism, which does not mean, of course, that there weren't those who made compromises. But resistance to the tendency to ideologize and politicize in literature, despite the occasional line penned to glorify Tito, lasted unusually long after the enemy, socialist realism, was dead and buried. There were many good writers, thanks to this, who wrote fine books; there were bad writers, on the other hand, who were labeled 'good' because they 'didn't get caught up in politics', just as many good writers were deemed bad because they had no bone to pick with the regime, or at least didn't do so publicly; and there were bad writers who were deemed good only because they had taken a public stand against the regime. The fine Croatian writer, Miroslav Krleža, long since dead and buried, bears a stigma to this day for his friendship with Tito.

Today, of course, I know that the connection between literature and 'ideology' has been around since the beginnings of literacy. The Bible is not only a grandiose literary work, but a grandiose ideological work. The history of the bond between literature and ideology is long, complex and dramatic. Writers have lost their lives because of the written word. The history of relations between emperors and poets, kings and court fools, those who commission literature and those who comply with the commissions is too gory, episodes of book burning and censorship too frequent, the number of writers' lives given for the freedom of speech, for an idea, or even just for a dream – is too vast to allow us to take this fatal *liaison* lightly. The notion of literary autonomy served too often as an alibi for it to enjoy full validity: when they thought they had something to gain by it, there were writers who stepped into politics; others took on politics even when doing so led to symbolic or real suicide. Some, when they looked to save their skins, sought the shield of literary autonomy, while others paid for their literary autonomy with their skins.

The tension between the two opposing poles – the political engagement of a writer and a writer's autonomy – was particularly dramatic in the literatures of the former Eastern Europe, and even today, surprising as this may seem, it has still not lost its hold, although the context has changed in terms of the politics, ideas and culture. Eastern European literary environments were much more rigid than Western European ones. In the Eastern European literary zones, careers were destroyed because of the written word, or conversely the writer was elevated to government president, minister or ambassador. This is no different today, though it may seem to be different: state institutions continue to play the part of literary patron, albeit a bad and stingy patron, but there is barely any independent territory left. The writer in small post-communist states is still treated as the 'voice of his people' or as a 'traitor'. Why? For the simple reason that communism in transitional countries has been replaced by nationalism, and both systems have their eyes on writers. The literary marketplace is too small for the writer to maintain his belief that he is independent.

There were many Yugoslav writers, who were not fortunate enough to survive the shift from socialism to nationalism, to re-position them-selves nationally, thereby insuring themselves a place on the bookshelves of the national literature. Some tried, and survived a year or so longer, slipping through the eye of the needle. Many of the losers, along with their collected works and mountains of scribbled pages, however, sank into the dust of oblivion. Young writers, and with them the young literary critics and scholars, showed no compassion, they must have figured this wasn't their story. Today is, after all, another time, life is proceeding at a rapid clip, literature is a time-investment which for most of us does not provide anything more than aching joints and bankruptcy, but it is a lottery which brings the lucky winner the jack pot. The young rush out to buy lottery tickets and don't ask too many questions.

How is it, for instance, that writers who were dissidents in their communist states are so quick to accept posts in ministries, embassies or elsewhere in the new democracies? How is it that today, in one way or another, everyone continues to live on government handouts? How is it that those who once pressed so fiercely for autonomy in literature are now demanding that their state institutions finance culture (hence literature), thereby implicitly agreeing that they won't bite the hand that feeds them? All in all, culture in small countries was never viable on the market, nor could it have been. That is why writers of small countries, whether they like it or not, are condemned to act as representatives for their country, whether the state be Croatia, Serbia,

Estonia, or Latvia, either that or they are labeled 'traitors' and live abroad. One often goes hand in hand with the other. Even international literary stars, which have long since left their home literatures behind and have changed the language they write in as they went, are not immune to the righteous fury of the homeland. The recent incident with Milan Kundera only confirms that the Czech republic is a small country, and that the model for the traumatic back-and-forth between literature and ideology is unchanged.

The question arises: is it possible to step out of the hellish circle, where the autonomy of a literary text might be another name for politicization, and politicization might be another name for autonomy? How does the relationship to a text change when the context changes?

Exile is a change of context in the literal sense. Exile implies the personal experience of every exiled writer, which would be difficult to subsume under the terms that are stubbornly endorsed by literary critics from the two worlds: the writer's home base and the hosting environment. The terms – *émigré, immigrant, exile, nomad, minority, ethnic* – are discriminatory, but also affirmative. With these terms the home base expels the writer, while the same terms are used by the host environment to thrust the writer into an ethnic niche, meanwhile affirming his or her existence. The home base makes assumptions of monoculturalism, xenophobia and exclusivity, while the host environment make assumptions of multiculturalism, cosmopolitanism and inclusivity, but both are essentially working with the dusty labels of ethnicity and the politics of *otherness*.

Even if I were to write a text about the desolation of frozen landscapes at the North Pole, I would still generally be labeled a Croatian writer, or a Croatian writer in exile writing about the desolation of the frozen landscapes at the North Pole. Reviewers would promptly populate the frozen wasteland of my text with concepts such as exile, Croatia, ex-Yugoslavia, post-communism, the Balkans, Eastern Europe, the Slavic world, Balkan feminism or perhaps Balkan eco-feminism, while journalists would ask me whether I had had the opportunity while up in the frozen wasteland to run into the Yugoslav Diaspora, and how I perceived the situation in Kosovo from the frozen point of view. If an English writer writes his or her version of a visit to the North Pole,

Englishness will not likely serve as the framework within which his or her text is read.

This attitude of the host environment to writer-newcomers springs from a subconscious colonial attitude, just when the larger literary world is doing its best to reject this; from a market which relishes any form of the profitable exotic; and from always vital relations between the periphery and the center. The concepts of periphery and center are, however, elastic; I am sure that Serbs feel closer to the center than do the Bulgarians and the Bulgarians feel closer to the center than do the Turks. Feelings, however, are one thing and real relations of power are something else. The real center of cultural power is America, or rather Anglo-American culture, whose cultural domination marked the twentieth century. We are still looking to that center with equal fascination today. Anglo-American culture is the dominant field of reference, while, at the same time, it is the most powerful, if not the most just, mediator of cultural values. In other words, if Chinese writers are not translated into English, it is unlikely that any Serbian or Croatian reader, with the exception of the occasional lone Sinologist, will ever hear of them.

The relationship to a literary text changes, of course, with the change of language. There are many examples of writers who embraced the language of their host-country, yet by doing so they did not manage to protect their texts from misreading. There are an even larger number of writers who, writing in the language of the host country, seek a special 'cultural' (which basically means ethnic or religious) status for them because only this status will make them visible. All in all, an opposition asserts itself here: this time the opposition between the autonomy of the literary text and its critical reception and market evaluation (the market not being without its political aspirations) in the new context of the internationalization of literary texts and transnational literature. This is still the realm of literature as we know it with its traditions, canons, apparatus, and institutions, with its system of values. This is a realm where literature (the same holds true of other cultural texts) is read and evaluated within gender and post-colonial coordinates too; within still existing bits and pieces of theoretical schools and approaches; within cultural geo-politics and its coordinates, such as Eastern European and Western European zones, or within the global cultural market dominated by American or Anglo-American language and culture. Here we still know, or at least we know approximately, what it is we are talking about when we speak of literature or culture.

As it leaps from the national to the international, literature enters its third, unavoidable context: a new epoch of digital revolution and globalization. In that context literature (and other cultural texts), or rather its assumptions, dissolve, vanish, or transmute into something else. True, the bookstores are full of books, the chains are reminiscent of supermarkets, there are more translations of books than ever before, more literary awards than ever, there are writers being lauded like pop stars, there are, for instance, rich networks of EU cultural institutions, managers, mediators and cultural bureaucracy, there are numerous cultural projects and events – all of which suggests that things have never been better for culture. However, the switch from Gutenberg to the Digital era caused a tectonic shift, and the impacts are much more serious and complicated than they seem, or than we are able to see, predict and articulate. The whole cultural system, with its codes, meanings, and language, disappeared or transmuted into something else. Cultural values and their hierarchy have been destroyed, differentiations and differences between popular and mass culture, and consequently high culture, do not exist today. Intellectuals and experts as arbiters have been pushed to the margins. Authors of works of art are disappearing together with the notion of authorship. A commonly known and oft-quoted fact is that the most consulted source of reference has become Wikipedia, an Internet encyclopedia made and controlled by anonymous kids. There is a whole parallel culture on the Internet with millions and millions of consumers, people who are not passive but ready to create, interact, to change, compile, to produce and exchange and, thanks to technology, they do so. Their main reference source is the huge industry of popular culture. And here is the paradox: thanks to sophisticated high tech devices we can observe the rapid process of regression and barbarization of culture. This is why the new consumer is not able to read and understand classical works of art any more (what the majority of us still consider culture), even if he would like to understand it. That is why we, on the other hand, are not able to communicate with the anonymous artistic production presented mostly on the Internet, on TV, but also in the written word, in books. The fact that celebrated David Hockney uses his iPhone to draw sketches does not slow the process, it rather he speeds it up.

Let us go back to the cultural zone we are all more comfortable with, to the regions local to Europe. Do we know what culture is or what culture is supposed to be? Is culture a sort of spiritual currency, a spiritual euro? Is culture a part of the national identity package? Is culture a part of the tourist industry (Let's build a museum of modern art. Once we have a museum we will find the art to furnish it, and once we have a furnished museum it will enrich our urban identity and provide us with the obligatory tourist magnet). What sort of cultural consumers do we produce and facilitate? Can we talk culture in Croatia, for instance (here I am using the transitional cultural pattern I know best), knowing at the same time that the whole education system has gone downhill? Can we talk culture if there is no reliable history textbook written in the lands of the former Yugoslavia (something that probably pertains to many other European countries as well)? Can we talk culture knowing that the Croatian Catholic Church has infiltrated schools and curricula? Or are we talking ideology here? Can we talk culture if the politics of the leading Croatian party, HDZ, has infiltrated the textbooks and even educational computer games? What type of cultural consumer are we raising if we find the name of Franjo Tudjman everywhere, even in the Croatian version of Monopoly? What type of cultural consumer are we raising if we find – in an educational computer game blessed by the Croatian Ministry of Culture – where the history of Dubrovnik was supposed to be, instead – a photo of a Ms. Suica, Dubrovnik's former mayor, a member, of course, of the HDZ party? Can we talk culture if just a decade or so ago there were cases of book burnings in Croatia, and the cleansing of Croatian libraries, blessed again by the Croatian Ministry of Culture. This manifestation of cultural vandalism, as far as I know, has never been written up in a report. More than that, I am certain the book burners are still employed, or happily retired. Can we talk culture, especially a border-free culture if, just a couple of years ago, culture was serving as a tool for creating borders? Can we talk culture if we know that many people of culture – writers, filmmakers, professors, intellectuals, and artists – were engaged themselves in the recent war machine as propagators and producers of hate speech? These same people are alive and well, holding jobs, having the cultural power to decide, censor, shape culture according to their tastes and their current political views. Moreover: such cultural commissars are often the loudest preachers of democracy. Can we talk culture if it is exclusively based on racial, national, ethnic and religious grounds? Can we talk culture in a society where the media are all in the hands of a few people, and censorship is worse than ever because it is not transparent? Can we talk culture in a society, which has disconnected itself from its own past, because it is not ready to confront and accept it?

So, what do we talk about when we talk culture? Are we equipped to answer that question? Add to this that we live in a new, self-centered epoch in which there is a premium on being heard rather than listening, being seen rather than watching, and on being read rather than reading. This new status of an author can be best explained by the image of a person who suffers at the same time from both autism and exhibitionism.

All in all, we are living in the ruins of the old cultural system. The crash of the system produced a terrible noise, and we are constantly exposed to it. We can no longer distinguish any more what it is we are hearing, and even if we hear something, we do not dare say and define it. Our language belongs to the old system. There is a vast army of facilitators of that noise, cultural critics, professors, educators, teachers, the cultural bureaucracy and many others, but nobody knows yet what the gist is of the noise.

Let us stop here and go back to the Wall. The hardest job after the fall of the Wall is not done yet, and this is the competent and relevant evaluation of what has been gained in the process and what has been lost. For this job we need scholars and thinkers who refuse to think within widely accepted stereotypes, political, ideological, cultural, and otherwise, and who have a sense of responsibility as robust as that of the good fellow, Telemachus. This is a job that should be done by all the sides, because *The Wall has fallen on everyone, on all of us,* as a friend of mine noticed a long time ago, with a tinge of melancholy in his voice.

Part II

Academic Discussion

The Temptation of National Identity: The Case of Grigor Părličev

Raymond Detrez

Abstract: Grigor Părličev (1831–1893), a Bulgarian from Ohrid, wrote his major works, the two epic poems *The Armatole* and *Skenderbeis*, during his stay in Athens as a student in the early 1860s. He then aspired to become a member of the Greek nation but never fully succeeded. In the late 1860s, back in Ohrid, he turned into a fierce Bulgarian nationalist. Eager to make a career as a Bulgarian writer, he translated the first chants of the *Iliad* and his own *The Armatole* into 'Common Slav'. However, due to his poor knowledge of literary Bulgarian he failed to be accepted by the Bulgarian cultural elite as one of them. The underlying reason of his failures might have been the fact that Părličev ultimately continued to identify himself with the pre-national multiethnic Orthodox Christian community in the Balkans rather than with a particular ethnic or national community. Thus Părličev remained all his life an outsider, whose position was comparable to a great extent to that of a writer in exile.
Keywords: Grigor Părličev, Bulgaria, Greece, national identity, Balkan mentality

Of all Balkan writers Grigor Părličev (1830–1893) is without any doubt the most authentically and completely *Balkanic*. Born in Ohrid in Macedonia in 1830 in a Slav speaking family, he wrote his major literary works – the two epic poems *The Armatole* (1860) and *Skenderbey* (1862) – in Greek.[1] The heroes of the first poem have Slav names, but according to what Părličev himself mentions in the notes added to the first printed edition, they are Albanians and Albanians are 'nothing else but Greeks' (Stavridhis 1985: 44). The main heroes of the second poem are pure-sang Albanians; the only Slav is a Montenegrin. In addition to these and a few other poems in archaizing Greek, Părličev wrote a number of didactic orations and poems for children in the dialect of his native town Ohrid, often using the Greek alphabet. His translations of Homer (published in *Čitalište* 1 (1870–1871), 11, 12, 13 and 16) and of his own *The Armatole* (Topalov 1980: 300–322) are written in a 'Common Slav language' he devised himself, while his *Autobiography* is penned in a language close to standard Bulgarian (Părličev 1980: 251–326). He continued writing poems, articles and letters in Greek until the end of his life. Although Pǎrličev did not write in Albanian and Turkish, it transpires from his *Autobiography* that he had a command of these languages as well.

Pǎrličev did not only know most of the Balkan languages, he also displayed a kind of Balkanic predisposition. Kiril Skopakov (1911: 477, 479) drew the attention to Pǎrličev's warm feelings for the various ethnic groups that populate the Balkan Peninsula. The *Autobiography*, he points out, offers an illustration

> of the simple customs of the Bulgarian population, the Turkish masses, and the Hellenized Bulgarian population. The author depicts in the same way the Bulgarian, the Turk, and the Greek, without being led by feelings of tribal and racist prejudices. For him, there are only human types and characters.
> [...]
> In general, the whole autobiography is a unique literary work, in which the customs and traditions of the three main populations of Macedonia, their racial particularities, their age-old conflicts and their fights for predominance are depicted with an objective simplicity. In this *Autobiography* wells up the love and the sympathy for the most downtrodden population.

Due to the multicultural aspects of his personality and his work, Pǎrličev has become the subject of an also very Balkanic debate on the issue to which national literature he properly belongs. As may be expected in the case of a Slav author born in Macedonia, the main claimants appear to be Bulgarian and Macedonian literary historians. Their difference of opinion, however, does not concern only Pǎrličev and, since the points of view are predictable, it is not particularly interesting, at least to an outsider. There is a less eye-catching, but actually far more interesting controversy on the issue whether at the time he wrote his great Greek poems Pǎrličev possessed a Greek or a Bulgarian national consciousness. Here Greek literary historians have their say as well. Although in 1862 *The Armatole* won the prestigious Athenian Poetry Contest, apart from a few references in the late 19th century (Rangabé 1877a and 1877b and Rangabé & Sanders 1884), Pǎrličev has not been included into general histories of Greek literature and has hardly been mentioned even in more comprehensive monographs. Bulgarian and Macedonian scholars tend to believe that this omission is deliberate and due to the role Pǎrličev played in the anti-Greek Bulgarian national movement in Ohrid in the 1860s and 1870s. A more probable explanation, however, is that Pǎrličev was in fact only a minor representative of the Athenian Romantic school which currently is almost completely forgotten as a whole because of its archaizing language and improbable sentimental and patriotic stories. Nevertheless, Titos Giochalas (1971), the former president of the Institute of Balkan Studies in Thessaloniki, did claim Părličev's Greek poems as a part of Greek literature.

Actually, what we deal with here is the rather trivial problem typical of a great part of emigrant literature as well: What is decisive to the issue as to which national literature a literary work actually belongs – the nationality of its author or the language in which it is written? A similar problem exists, at least for Macedonian literary historians, in relation to the *Autobiography* and other texts Părličev wrote in (some sort of) standard Bulgarian: Do they belong to Bulgarian literature, because they are written in Bulgarian, or to Macedonian literature, because Părličev (to them) is a Macedonian?

Not only Părličev's literary work raises a number of problems characteristic of emigrant literature. Părličev himself in many respects shared the fate of an emigrant writer (cf. Detrez 2007). In the Balkans, feelings of estrangement and homesickness do not seem to require a long distance from one's native town or village. The Greek songs of *xenitia (sojourning abroad)* suggest that one can feel an emigrant or immigrant on the nearby island or in the neighbouring village. As an 'emigrant', Părličev spent about half of his adult life residing in various places all over the Balkans – either outside (or almost outside) the Slav ethnic zone properly speaking – in Tirana, Istanbul, Thessaloniki – or outside the Ottoman Empire, the state whose resident he was – in Athens, which at the time of his stay was the capital of the Kingdom of Greece, and Sofia, the capital of the autonomous principality of Bulgaria. In his speech on the occasion of the Day of the HH. Cyrillus and Methodius in Thessaloniki (probably) in 1885, Părličev addressed the Bulgarian teachers attending the celebration, thanking them for having come 'from their fatherland' (the Principality of Bulgaria) to 'our fatherland' (still Ottoman Macedonia) (Părličev 1980: 232). We learn from his *Autobiography* that, when staying abroad, Părličev often suffered from nostalgia. Recalling his stay in Tirana in 1848, he wrote: "I was seized with nostalgia (the homeland illness): I was eighteen years old and abroad for the first time. Especially during the night, I wept for my mother for hours" (Părličev 1980: 270). Commenting on his stays in other places, Părličev does not refer to his homesickness so explicitly, but he rarely felt comfortable. There was always something to complain about. Living in the Vlach village in Dolna Belica as a teacher in the 1850s, he was enthusiastic about the beautiful scenery of the village; however, the 'Belica society' soon started irritating him (Părličev 1980: 275). Many years later, Părličev experienced similar negative feelings during his stay in Bulgaria in 1879–1880. Employed as a teacher in Gabrovo, Părličev complains about "the roughness of the local climate" and "the local dialect" which he was not able to master (Părličev 1980, 389, in a letter to Konstantin Jireček). Later, Părličev worked as a librarian in the National Library, then housed in the Big Mosque (now the Archaeological Museum) in Sofia – "a dark and moist building" he soon left as well (Părličev 1980: 325).

Obviously, Părličev felt somehow better in Athens, where he spent in total six years of his life, from 1849 to 1852 and from 1859 to 1862. Many facts indicate that he was relatively well integrated in Greek society and there is little doubt about Părličev's preparedness to become a full-fledged 'Hellene'. The two short poems he published in 1859 in Athens apropos a quarrel he had in the Russian church reveal him as a fierce anti-Slavic Greek nationalist (Kadach 1971). In 1860, after *The Armatole* was awarded the first prize at the Poetry Contest, Alexandhros Rangavis, the president of the jury, praised him in his report as the living evidence of the presence of Greek culture in an area as remote as Northern Macedonia.[2] For a couple of months Părličev was a national celebrity. The well-known Greek writer Emmanouil Roidhis requested him to translate Chateaubriand in Greek (Papastathis 1972–1973: 155–9). As usual, however, the jury's decision was contested by a part of the literary critics and the public. During the ensuing debate, his opponent, the poet and professor of botany at the University, Theodhoros Orphanidhis, also brought up Părličev's position of a Bulgarian, residing in Athens, maliciously suggesting (in *Avgi* (*Dawn*) from 7 May 1860) that Părličev was 'a tool of Bulgarian propaganda' in Greece. In spite of the Greek feelings Părličev had demonstrated on several occasions and in spite of the eagerness of the majority of the Greek nationalist cultural elite to adopt him as one of them, Părličev often felt a stranger, excluded from the society he wanted to be a part of. Together with the ambition to merge the many Balkan ethnic groups into the Greek nation, there existed among the Greeks also a considerable racist bias against them. Părličev found "pride" (*gordost*) in every word of his fellow students;

because of his pronunciation and his poverty, he felt treated "with contempt" (*prezritelno*) (Părličev 1980: 273). Whether this disdainful attitude of the Greeks was real or imagined does not matter much. The way Părličev felt he was treated seems to be very similar to the way many well integrated migrants in Western Europe and elsewhere feel to be treated nowadays by the communities they want to be a member of.

Tragically, Părličev went through a similar traumatic event after the publication in the Bulgarian literary review *Čitalište* (*Reading Room*) in 1870–1871 of his translation of the first chants of Homer's *Iliad* into his self-devised 'Common Slav language'. The outstanding critic Nešo Bončev (1983: 108–9) with good reason blamed Părličev for having no command of Bulgarian and for using certain phonetic and lexical features of the Macedonian dialects. According to Bončev, Părličev had produced a translation that did not meet the most elementary artistic requirements. In addition to the inappropriate use of his archaic 'Common Slav language', Părličev had replaced Homer's hexameter by the metre of the South Slav epic songs and had abridged the chants whenever he judged them too long-drawn-out. Some of the most authoritative Bulgarian writers of his time ridiculed the translation. In his satirical poem *Why I'm not?* (Zašto ne săm), Hristo Botev (1979: 49) wrote:

Why I'm not Părličev?
I would translate the Iliad;
but for that translation,
I would deserve a trashing.

And Ljuben Karavelov (1985: 189) compared Părličev to "an empty pumpkin".

Although eager – as a former Greek poet and a Bulgarian national revival activist – to be accepted now as a genuine Bulgarian writer, Părličev was rudely excluded from Bulgarian literary life, not only because of his clumsy translation, but also – which was even more offensive – because of his ignorance of the Bulgarian language. Părličev had left Athens in 1862, affronted, if we may believe his *Autobiography*, by the Greeks' disdain for the Bulgarians. In 1889, after having attempted repeatedly – in his *Dream of an Old Man* (1883) and his *Autobiography* (1884) – to prove his loyalty to the Bulgarian nation, he resentfully signed one of his writings with

"Grigor Părličev, killed by the Bulgarians (*ubitij bolgarami*)" (Arnaudov 1927: 1079). For the second time, Părličev's efforts to be accepted by the national community he identified himself with were shattered. In both cases he remained an outsider.

At this point, Părličev might have developed a Macedonian identity, as some other intellectuals in Macedonia did, but there are in fact no clear indications this happened. By the end of his life, the community Părličev identified himself with seems to have been narrowed to the inhabitants of Ohrid and its surroundings. Probably, it is a normal psychological development for an aging man to return to his native town and spend there the last years of his life, displaying a particular devotion to the community he had been a part of from his early childhood. However, as the Bulgarian historian Hristo Gandev (1976: 736) argued, the perception of the 'fatherland' as limited to one's native town or village and the broader region where it is located in is typical of a Mediaeval, pre-national(ist) perception of the world and goes hand in hand with an individual's identification with a religious instead of an ethnic community. This pre-national mental make-up existed in the Balkans until the late 19th century.[3] As all people in the Balkans at that time, Părličev was raised in this pre-national(ist) spirit. Before being exposed to the temptation of various nationalisms, he must have felt a member of the Balkan Orthodox Christian community in the first place. The two epic poems he wrote in Athens are impregnated with the corresponding 'Balkan mentality'. Significantly, Părličev does not mention in them any ethnic, let alone national communities opposing each other, but only religious communities – Christians and Muslims (Detrez 1990).

One might argue that Părličev actually has remained a representative of this pre-national Balkan Orthodox mentality until the end of his life. Living in the age when nationalism captured the minds, he could not help paying tribute to this forceful new ideology. To many people in the 19th century (and later) – artists, scholars, politicians, soldiers –, not only in the Balkans, but all over the globe, nation and nation-state building offered new opportunities for material and spiritual self-achievement. Părličev twice attempted to realize himself in the field first of Greek and later of Bulgarian national literature. Due to unfavourable circumstances or to his insufficient command of the appropriate social strategies, he twice failed. In Athens he was accepted as a writer, but ultimately not as a Greek; in

Sofia he was probably accepted as a Bulgarian, but by no means as a writer.

We will not go deeper into Părličev's personal tragedy, but focus on the pre-national Orthodox Christian mental make-up we referred to, as it offers us a view on what might possibly be a non-national consciousness. People in the 21st century, even if they are no nationalists, nevertheless tend to consider national identity as an essential component of their identities as a human beings. Many writers and other intellectuals in the Balkans and elsewhere recently embarked on finding a sort of middle way between nationalism, which they reject, and the nurturing of a national identity as something particularly precious and almost a prerequisite of mental health. However, as historians know (or should know), from the dawn of mankind until the end of the 18th century a state of mind which could be labelled a 'national consciousness' did not exist. Although people were aware of their own and others' belonging to specific ethnic groups, they considered ethnic affiliation as irrelevant to whatever really matters in life.

The Balkan Orthodox Christian cultural community Părličev belonged to surfaced under Ottoman rule and disintegrated as a result of the emergence of ethnic nationalism in the 19th century. It continued the Byzantine commonwealth, but as a result of its long existence within the borders of the Ottoman Empire, it acquired a number of specific features, unknown to Russian Orthodoxy and typical of the social, political and spiritual traditions of the Patriarchy of Constantinople: the multi-ethnic character of its clergy, the use of Greek as a liturgical language, the language of church administration and consequently as a *lingua communa*, the 'geography of faith' covering the whole empire. Members of the Orthodox community – not systematically, but frequently – called themselves 'Romaeans' (*romei*, that means Romans, or Byzantines, or Orthodox Christians). Ethnonyms like 'Greek', 'Bulgarian', 'Vlach', 'Arnaut' were used to denote ethnic groups, but referred in many instances also to religious groups – 'Greek' as a synonym of 'Orthodox Christian' and 'Turk' in the sense of 'Muslim' as is common in many Balkan languages even today – or to social or vocational groups. In 19th-century Bulgarian, 'Greek' could also mean 'city-dweller' or 'trader'. A 'Vlach' could be everyone, of whatever ethnic origin, engaged in semi-nomadic cattle breeding. Apparently, since the basic community individuals identified themselves with was of a religious and not of an ethnic nature, unambiguous ethnic denominations obviously were regarded as irrelevant.

The Balkan Orthodox Christian community developed one single, common high culture, which was predominantly religious until the end of the 18th century when many of his members embraced the French Enlightenment – a development which is reflected in Părličev's work as well, in particular in his orations to the churchgoers in Ohrid in the 1860s and the 1870s (Părličev 1980: 195–237). Most Balkan literature, whether religious or enlightened, was written in learned, archaizing Greek, which was the common language of intellectual communication of the Orthodox Christian community. The authors of these books were overwhelmingly Greeks, but also Albanians, Bulgarians, Greeks, Romanians and Vlachs, writing for an equally ethnically mixed audience of readers. We know the names of about thirty Bulgarian authors who wrote in Greek (Nikolova 2006: 109). Even more impressive was the number of Bulgarian readers of Greek books. From 1750 to 1840 not less than 1115 Greek printed books (titles, not copies) circulated in Bulgaria and only 52 Bulgarian ones (Stojanov 1957: 471–2; Stojanov 1978: 47–168). This is no indication of Bulgarian 'cultural backwardness': In the framework of the Orthodox Christian community, Greek books apparently satisfied the Bulgarian intellectual and educational needs. As there were books in demotic (spoken) Greek for those who did not understand learned, archaizing Greek, there were also books in 'demotic' Bulgarian – the *damaskini* – for those Bulgarians who did not understand Greek. (At variance with learned Greek, the use of Church Slavonic was limited almost exclusively to the religious sphere.)

In the light of the Balkan Orthodox Christian community, many obscure or contradictory aspects of the life and work of Grigor Părličev become understandable. Părličev wrote in Greek, because Greek was the language of the community he addressed. His audience was not a Greek, but a multiethnic Orthodox Christian audience. As his correspondence with the Robev family in Ohrid shows, Părličev took great care to sell the printed version of *The Armatole* all over the Balkan Peninsula, and not only in Greece or among the Greeks (Părličev 1980: 351–4). In the framework of the Balkan community, it was not strange for a Slav to write in Greek about Albanians and not to make precise distinctions between ethnic groups. These distinctions seem to have been neither clear nor important to Părličev. Having been tempted by Greek ethnic nationalism, he finally broke with it as soon as he understood that he would never feel and never be treated as an ethnic Greek. As the turning point, literary historians consider the moment when Părličev, still in Athens, learned about the death of Dimităr Miladinov, which was blamed on the Greek clergy. At that juncture, however, to Părličev Dimităr Miladinov was not yet a champion of Bulgarian nationalism, but the adored Slav teacher who introduced him into the Greek language and literature. His troubled relations with both the Greeks and the Bulgarians suggest that Părličev probably fitted into no ethnic or national community at all. After the Orthodox Christian community was replaced with communities marked by ethnic nationalism, be it Greek or Bulgarian, Părličev had become an 'emigrant' in a particular sense of the word: A person who did not move to another country, but feels alienated and confused in his or her own country the moral, religious, political and aesthetic value systems of which have radically changed.

History teaches us that in the past many societies have been based not on ethnicity as a source of commonality and solidarity, but on religion – as was the case of the Balkan Orthodox Christian community we discussed here – or on a secular ideology as, for instance, Enlightenment and civil nationalism. To many of our contemporaries, obsessed with national identity, it often looks as if a person's loyalty to that kind of ethnically unmarked communities has something artificial. However, why should Părličev's early identification with and loyalty to the supra-ethnic Orthodox Christian community in the Ottoman Empire be an aberration – a *zabluda* or *zabluždenie*, as it has often been called? Did his adopting an ethnic Greek or Bulgarian identity make him a better, more authentic and more complete human being? Should his choice to write in the language of the Balkan Orthodox Christian community be branded as an expression of disloyalty to his own community? Should an artistic creation necessarily radiate an ethnic or national identity? And is a writer obliged to stay true to his or her native language – or even his native community – forever and ever? Recently, the German linguist Christian Voss (2006: 99) wondered whether "the right of languages" (to be protected from extinction) "prevail over the rights of speakers to adapt competitively to new socioeconomic ecologies". Should not writers have the right to 'adapt competitively' as well by opting for another language than their native one, without being blamed or blaming themselves therefore?

These are a few questions which came to my mind when I was reflecting, with a view to this conference, on the life and work of Grigor Părličev. His tragic personality bears a number of features from a pre-national(ist) world which was lost in the turmoil of nationalisms and which we now attempt to recreate in a different way through European integration – in conditions of a re-emerging fixation on national identity though which would probably be very recognizable to Părličev.

Notes

[1] *The Armatole* was first published in Athens in 1860 (facsimile edition: Stavridhis 1985). A Bulgarian translation included into Părličev 1980: 29–61; a Macedonian translation (with a facsimile edition of the Greek text) in Prličev 1983. The Greek text of *Skenderbeis* was published for the first time, with a Bulgarian, respectively Macedonian translation, in Părličev 1967 and Prličev 1974.
[2] Published in *Pandhora* (on May 1, 1860, 53–4). See the Macedonian, resp. Bulgarian translation in Petruševski (1980: 20–25) and Topalov (1982: 51–4).
[3] For the Balkan Orthodox Christian community, see Kitromilides (2007: I) and Detrez (2008).

Bibliography

Arnaudov, Michail. 1927. 'Григор Пърличев (1830–1893)' in *Училищен преглед* 26: 1063–81.
Bončev, Nešo. 1983. *Съчинения*. София: Български писател.
Botev, Christo. 1979. *Събрани съчинения*. vol. 1. София: Български писател.
Detrez, Raymond. 1990. 'От религиозно до национално съзнание. Няколко наблюдения върху националното самоосъзнаване на Балканите' in *Литертурна мисъл* 34(5): 64–78.
— 2007. '"There I was seized with nostalgia." Migration, nostalgia and nationalism in the Bulgarian National Revival Period' in Zhivko Ivanov *et al.* (eds). *Migration, Modern Nationalism and Nostalgia in the Age of Globalization*. Plovdiv: Plovdiv University Press: 145–60.
— 2008. 'Език и литература на "ромейската" общност' in *Slavica Gandensia* 35: 37–64.
Gandev, Christo. 1976. *Проблеми на Българското Възраждане*. София: Наука и изкуство.
Giochalas, Titos. 1971. 'Τὸ ἐπικὸν ποίημα τοῦ ἐξ Ἀχρίδου Γρηγορίου Σταυρίδου (Prličev) "Σκενδέρμπεης". Ἱστορικαὶ καὶ λογοτεχνικαὶ πηγαὶ' in *Μακεδονικά* 11: 174–259.
Kadach, Dorothea. 1971. 'Zwei griechische Gedichte von Grigor S. Prličev (Γρηγόριος Σταυρίδης)' in *Ἑλληνικά* 24: 107–15.
— 1971–1972. 'Die Polemik Orphanidis–Prličev anläßlich des Athener Dichterwettbewerbs 1860' in *Zeitschrift für Balkanologie* 8(1–2): 84–100.

Karavelov, Ljuben. 1985. *Събрани съчинения*. vol. 5. София: Български писател.

Kitromilides, Paschalis. 2007. 'Orthodox Culture and Collective Identity in the Ottoman Balkans during the Eighteenth Century' in Kitromilides, Paschalis. *An Orthodox Commonwealth. Symbolic Legacies and Cultural Encounters in Southeastern Europe*. Aldershot: Ashgate (Variorum), I.

Nikolova, Nadka. 2006. *Билингвизмът в българските земи през XV–XIX век*. Шумен: Шуменски университет Епископ 'Констнтин Преславски'.

Papastathis, Ch. 1972–1973. 'Grigor Părličev traducteur de Chateaubriand en Grec' in *Cyrillomethodianium* 2: 155–9.

Părličev, Grigor. 1967. *Скендербей*. (translation Hristo Kodov). София: БАН.

— 1980. *Избрани произведения*. София: Български писател.

Prličev, Grigor. s.d. *Скендербеj*. (translation Mihail Petruševski). Скопjе: Македонска книга.

— 1983. *Мартолозот*. (translation Mihail Petruševski).

Petruševski, Michail. 1980. 'А. Р. Рангавис за поезиjата на Г. С. Прличев и неговото место во литературата' in *Беседи за Прличев*. Скопjе: Гоце Делчев.

Rangabé, Alexandre. 1877a. *Histoire littéraire de la Grèce moderne*. Paris: Calmann Lévy.

— 1877b. *Précis d'une histoire de la littérature néo-hellénique*. Berlin: S. Calvary & Cie.

— and Daniel Sanders. 1884. *Geschichte der neugriechischen Literatur*. Leipzig: Wilhem Friedrich.

Skopakov, Kiril. 1911. 'Григор С. Пърличев' in *Известия на Семинара по славянска филология при Университета в София* 3: 413–94.

Stern, Dieter and Christian Voss (eds). 2006. "Towards the peculiarities of language shift in Northern Greece". In: *Marginal Linguistic Identities. Studies in Slavic Contact and Borderland Varieties*. (Eurolinguistische Arbeiten 3). Wiesbaden: Harrassowitz Verlag: 87–101.

Stojanov, Manjo. 1959. *Българска възрожденка книжнина*. vol. 1. София: Наука и изкуство.

— 1973. *Опис на гръцките и други чиждоезични ръкописи в Народната библиотека 'Кирил и Методий'*. София: Наука и изкуство.

— 1978. *Стари гръцки книги в България*. София: Народна библиотека 'Кирил и Методий'.

Topalov, Kiril. 1982. *Григор Пърличев — живот и дело*. София: Български писател.

Bulgarian Émigrés and Their Literature:
A Gaze from Home

Nikolaj Aretov

Abstract: The paper sketches the general picture of literature written far from home in the late 20th and early 21st century. Noting three *waves* of Bulgarian writers living abroad and the dynamics of their work, the author focuses on the reception of this kind of literature at home – demonized and mythologized, rejected and perceived as forbidden fruit, and political analysis. The language used in such literature is also scrutinized from the point of view of the *exoticism* of a Bulgarian text published in a foreign context, or the legitimization of a text originally published in a foreign language. The author illustrates his observation with the reception of the work of a number of Bulgarian émigré writers.

Keywords: Émigré writers, three waves of emigration, reception at home, demonized and mythologized.

The terms *émigré* and *émigré literature* seem clear and unambiguous only at first glance. Although the differences are not always important or visible, there are clear distinctions among the descriptors *emigrant*, *migrant*, and *diaspora*. It is even more critical to distinguish between literature written and published first in the language of the country of the writer's birth (literature targeted chiefly at readers that recognize this language as their 'own') and literature written in the language of the country where the writer, as emigrant, has made his or her new home (and targeted at new readers). Continuing in this vein, one could ask whether literature published in the native language targets a 'native' public or deliberately marks itself as exotic with all the implications that postcolonial criticism highlights. The films of Sarajevo-born Serbian filmmaker Emir Kusturica offer a clear instance of the instrumental use of Balkan exoticism. On the other hand, examples abound in which publication in the language of the adopted country is seen as a route to gaining authority that will then legitimize an author for his or her native readers.

In tandem with this kind of questioning about the language in which writers think and write go queries about the values that have shaped a particular piece of literature. Relatively speaking, questions about the plots and subjects of literature written abroad matter less. In some cases, plots are *native*, in others, plots represent the new environment in which the émigré author lives. Things become more complicated when we bear in mind that some works incorporate foreign plots even when written by authors in their native country, or having returned to their native country after a short sojourn abroad. The return of a writer who was a temporary or permanent emigrant also influences reception.

Bulgaria has a long but not particularly well known tradition of émigré literature (Karabelova 1996). From the early nineteenth century onward, important contributors to Bulgarian literature lived and wrote outside predominantly Bulgarian ethnic and linguistic territories. Mount Athos, Istanbul, Odessa, and Brăila all became significant centers of Bulgarian cultural activity. Many of the texts produced in those centers were written in other languages but were and are perceived as belonging to the Bulgarian cultural heritage. Historical and journalistic works published in Russia and in Russian generated important debates among Bulgarian speakers and had their champions and detractors before the new Bulgarian state was established in 1878. For example, Lyuben Karavelov's early works originally written or published in Russian are considered an integral part of Bulgarian literature. Generally speaking, works written in Greek had fewer readers and met with a varied reception: the poems of Grigor Părličev were perceived as Bulgarian, while those of Nikola Pikolo were not. Writers based in Rumania also met with a varied reception. If they wrote in Bulgarian, their works became part of the body of Bulgarian literature. If they wrote in Rumanian (as for example D. Veliksin) their work was perceived as peripheral to the shaping of a Bulgarian national literature. Journalistic texts in French were not perceived as highly prestigious even when they embraced the canonic vision of Bulgarian history.

After Bulgaria won its independence from the Ottoman Empire in 1878, a great number of émigrés returned home. The importance of literature produced abroad diminished; yet émigré literature remained responsible for introducing new ideas and stylistic trends to the new Bulgarian state as censorship weakened. (Many historians tend to exaggerate and even demonize Ottoman censorship vis-à-vis that of Imperial Russia or the Patriarchate of Constantinople).

For a relatively short period during the rule of Stefan Stambolov (1887–1894) some well-known authors emigrated, mostly voluntarily, including Ivan Vazov and Konstantin Veličkov. While abroad, they wrote works that entered the Bulgarian canon quickly (for example, the most popular and appreciated Bulgarian novel *Pod Igoto* (*Under the Yoke*) by Ivan Vazov, and others became part of the corpus of Bulgarian literature (Veličkov's *Pisma ot Rim* [*Letters from Rome*, 1895] and *Carigradski soneti* [*Istanbul Sonnets*, 1899]). The simple fact that these texts were written abroad was relatively unimportant for their reception.

In the first part of the twentieth century, there were more Bulgarian writers working outside Bulgaria but writing in Bulgarian. Among them were such prominent authors as Kiril Christov, Jordan Jovkov, Atanas Dalčev[1], Vladimir Poljanov, Svetoslav Minkov, and Elisaveta Bagriana. These writers worked abroad for various reasons. Some of them attended foreign universities or went to study contemporary culture; some were voluntary exiles; others were economic migrants. But once again their émigré status was not relevant to the reception of their work among Bulgarian readers. Their sojourn abroad was simply intended to expand their cultural horizons. Almost all of them introduced plots, figures, and personal impressions from abroad more frequently than authors from the previous generations had done.

After World War II significant changes occurred in the field of émigré literature. In the Bulgarian context, we can observe several 'waves' of emigrants. The first short wave, which came immediately after 1944, was predominantly political: few writers emigrated in this period, which was chiefly an exodus of journalists. The second, longer wave consisted of a constant but not so numerous stream of writers and intellectuals who left Bulgaria in the period from 1950 to 1985. Some left for political reasons; others were motivated by economic opportunities. Some intellectuals sought fulfillment of professional ambition at European and American universities. The third and most numerous wave dates from 1985 onwards. It was facilitated by Mikhail Gorbachev's *Perestroika* and gained momentum after the fall of the Berlin Wall in 1989. Migrants of the third wave were younger, less motivated by political events, and more likely to take advantage of economic and educational opportunities. Among them there are many university lecturers who wrote fiction or poetry.

Curiously, Bulgarian literature abroad was written, in the past, in Imperial Russia, in Western and Central Europe, and in the Balkans, but not in the Soviet Union, despite the presence of a relatively large group of political emigrants there, especially after 1923. This trend has expanded in recent decades beyond to include some members of the old diaspora who have become more active. In the early 21st century, Bulgarian literature is being written mostly in Western Europe, North America, and elsewhere, but not much of it in Eastern Europe (despite a large migration of Bulgarian intellectuals in Poland and the Czech Republic) or in the Balkans. One of the few exceptions is the poet Jana Bukova who lives in Greece and translates extensively from Bulgarian to Greek and vice versa.

This paper would not be complete without at least a mention of three important groups which I do not plan to discuss in this survey: ethnic Bulgarians living in Serbia, the Banat, Moldavia, and Ukraine represent an interesting group of writers from earlier diasporas who have recently become more active in publications for non-literary reasons. Some of those from the Jewish diaspora who settled in Israel after 1948 were or became writers and continue to contribute to Bulgarian literature, as do Bulgarian Turks who emigrated following the so-called Regeneration Processes of the 1980s.

Relationships between representatives of the different waves are charged with tensions and conflicts that arise from generational divisions, aesthetic differences, and, lastly, political rivalries.

Attitudes in Bulgaria toward emigrants and émigré literature are no less complex. The factors that determine attitudes and reception are not so radically different from the factors that determine attitudes towards the reception of all literary texts. First, readers must have access to the texts produced by émigré writers. In this respect literature written abroad is still at a disadvantage vis-à-vis literature written at home. Here there are at least four relevant factors. First, the text should be published and then properly distributed. Second, the reading public must be able to shape the émigré author and his or her text into a myth or story. This political, non-literary factor is important for readers. Third, the reaction of critics, the media, and state propaganda may or may not affect the perception of the readers and the reception of the literary work. Finally, the reading public is very diverse. Are the readers members of the émigré circle abroad, are they readers back home in the native country, do they represent a third group of émigrés more widely spread abroad, are they drawn from a larger, general international audience or an audience in the adopted homeland of the émigré-turned-immigrant? How do the different perspectives of the readers (recipients) affect readership and reception?

Attitudes toward emigrants and émigré literature are a dynamic process. Before 1989 the official propaganda in Bulgaria systematically and intentionally demonized emigrants and rejected even the possibility that émigré writers could produce high-quality literature. State propaganda evolved during the period from 1944 to 1989 and successfully forged and maintained this constant myth about the emigrants until the collapse of communism. Nevertheless one should not overestimate its effect, because this myth had its mirror-image created by the Bulgarian broadcasts of Radio Free Europe, the BBC, and, to a lesser extent, the Voice of America. Official Bulgarian state propaganda was also frequently counter-productive. It often produced unintended consequences and undesired results. (This is not only a Bulgarian or Balkan phenomenon.) Consequently, a heroic counter-myth about emigrants and their literature evolved in Bulgaria. Both types of myth (the demonized and the heroic) are more the result of propaganda than of a real understanding of emigrant literature.

The case of Tzenko Barev offers a curious illustration of the fragility of the myth jointly forged by official propaganda and counter-propaganda. Barev was the leader of the Agrarian Party abroad, presented as a man whom even Todor Živkov feared. Returning to Bulgaria, Barev immediately occupied a central place in politics, ran for the presidency but was soon marginalized. His last appearance on the political stage was an attempt to be elected as village mayor, in which he also failed.

Things become even more complicated if one considers the psychological context of writing in emigration. It is quite possible that émigré writers fear they will not be fully understood by their compatriots simply because they are emigrants. On the other hand, there are émigré writers who believe that their position in itself invests them with some kind of 'truth'. Inevitably such attitudes generate negative reactions and adversely affect the reception of this literature.

Some *forbidden* books have enjoyed eager reception. The most popular were hardly Bulgarian texts and surely not novels or poems written abroad. Readers in Bulgaria were most drawn to memoirs, such as, for example, those of Ivan (Vanče) Mihailov, leader of the Internal Macedonian Revolutionary Organization. Political journalism was also popular, as was the work of Bulgarians, published while they were still at home and then when they were subsequently banished the work gained popularity – for example, the early books of Georgi Markov. The phenomenon of the real reception of forbidden books in the late 20th century remains an unexplored topic. Yet it seems to me that most popular were old, occult books, for example, the lectures of Peter Dănov, memoirs, Russian novels (mainly Aleksandr Solženitsyn), old romances (not exactly banned, but out-of-print), old or new erotic literature (mostly translations, but some Bulgarian too), old or even recently written apocrypha, foreign novels from the United States and Western Europe, memoirs of Bulgarian victims of communism (mainly communists!) often published copies of radio broadcasts. Émigré novels, short stories, and poems come at the end of this long list.

The difficulty in distinguishing among different types of reception – abroad and at home, that of the general public and the authorities or experts (literary critics, journalists, state propagandists, etc) – is rendered more complicated when the topic is émigré literature. The same holds true for changes in the reception over time. The most obvious changing point was the fall of the Berlin wall in 1989. It is relatively easy to notice the difference between critical reviews and later studies and essays in the field of the history of literature, but the dynamic is much more complex. The most important factor, of course, is the political relationship between author and recipient. As a rule, readers appreciate the work of an author who holds the same political affiliation more readily than that of a political opponent or enemy. On the other hand, the work of opponents generates more noisy reactions.

In the late 20th century, particularly after the start of Mikhail Gorbachev's *Perestroika* (1985), Bulgarians began to rethink their attitude toward emigrants. The Internet and the whole revolution in access to information had a serious impact on this process. Changing receptions can be traced in several locations – the mass media, academic criticism, Wikipedia and other web sites (sometimes created with the participation of the émigré authors themselves), and various internet forums. The shift in official propaganda after 1989 toward greater acceptance of emigrants had a complex effect that included positive reactions but also specific kinds of frustration and envy. These reactions were (and are) often not articulated, not admitted, and not even conscious; and they exist not only among individuals affiliated in some way with the *ancient régime* but with others as well.

The *Dictionary of New Bulgarian Literature* prepared by the Institute for Literature (Bulgarian Academy of Sciences) and published in the early 1990s aimed at revising the idea of Bulgarian literature. One of its accents was on attitudes toward emigrants. One interesting sentence in the brief introduction, signed 'From the Editorial Board', was clearly the result of a compromise reached between the different members of the board. It was evidence of changing attitudes, strikingly old-fashioned language, unspoken limitations, and a problematic list of representatives of émigré literature:

> Речникът съдържа статии за представители на българската поезия, проза и наука като Стефан Груев, Христо Огнянов, Петър Увалиев, Юлия Кръстева, Цветан Тодоров, Атанас Славов и други, чието дело е влог в развитието на чуждестранните култури, но носи отпечатъка и на патриотичната съпричастност към българската проблематика, белязано със знака на автобиографизма.
>
> (This Dictionary contains articles about representatives of Bulgarian poetry, fiction, and science, such as Stephane Groueff, Hristo Ognjanov, Peter Uvaliev, Julia Kristeva, Tzvetan Todorov, Atanas Slavov, and others whose work is a contribution to the development of foreign cultures but bears the stamp of patriotic participation in Bulgarian problems marked by the sign of autobiographic narration). (Šiškova, 1994: 5)

Western radio stations broadcasting in the Bulgarian language played a crucial role in promoting first- and second-wave emigrants to the Bulgarian public. Each radio station – *BBC*, *Radio Free Europe*, *Voice of America*, *Deutsche Welle* – had its specific choice and was part of a propaganda apparatus while becoming the object of fierce counter-propaganda that actually bolstered its popularity in Bulgaria. The stations did not devote much air time to literature but their emigrant programmers and speakers offered critical reviews of editions in Bulgaria. Emigrants established their reputation there as journalists and critics but not as writers of *high* literature. In the 1950s and 1960s, differentiation between *high* and *popular* culture was rock hard and rarely problematized in Bulgaria.

On the other hand, the academic disciplines of literature and history provided the most powerful sources of authority and acceptance for first-wave emigrants, particularly in Germany. The Bulgarian academic society *Petăr Beron* was one of the most recognized organizations among academics. Established in Munich in the 1960s, it published Bulgarian Yearbooks in German. Official Bulgarian scholarship did not refer to these studies, which nonetheless had their small and enthusiastic group of adherents.

Hristo Ognjanov (1911–1997) stands out among first-wave emigrants who had ambitions to produce *high* literature. Ognjanov used the pen-name Boris Bosilkov when he wrote as a journalist, thus clearly separating *high* from *popular* literature. His ambitions for high literature reached Bulgarian readers after the Changes (1989) when some collections of his verses were published in Bulgaria, both in Bulgarian and in bilingual Bulgarian–German editions. The strategy of these editions was to suggest that they were not something new but rather recognized masterpieces, even classical works. In similar editions, poems were published side by side with other texts, for example, interviews, memoirs, and introductions by other emigrants or eminent scholars. Ognjanov's verses acquired some prestige but were hardly popular and did not find their way into academic studies on Bulgarian literature. Despite their striving for universal values, they have not enjoyed broader reception outside the Bulgarian reading public. Ognjanov's memoirs are relatively more popular (Ognjanov 1992, 1995a etc.)

Stefan Popov (1906–1989) was another first-wave emigrant who lived in Germany. Unlike Ognjanov, he had no literary ambitions. His first book was published in Bulgaria before World War II (Popov 1938). After the Changes, which he did not live to see, several of his books, translated from the German, were published in Bulgaria (Popov 1992, 1994, 1999). Although they are not widely popular, they are valued by a not-so-well-defined group of new Bulgarian conservatives who see him as "*the greatest Bulgarian thinker on a European scale*".

Peter Uvaliev (Pierre Rouve, 1915–1999) enjoyed a remarkable career abroad and is particularly highly appreciated in Bulgaria, and, moreover, not on political grounds. Uvaliev was first and foremost a cultural figure – a journalist, screenwriter, film producer, essayist, and art historian. He was the first emigrant to visit Bulgaria officially, personally invited by Lyudmila Živkova, the daughter of the former communist dictator. He was an extremely eloquent man, and his popularity was due mainly to the lectures and interviews he gave during his visit. After the Changes, Uvaliev and a number of other emigrants received apologies from several quarters, including groups close to the former Communist Party. In such cases, the quest for legitimacy goes both ways.

 Stephen Groueff (1922–2006) was the author of what is arguably the most popular book written by a first-wave emigrant. His *Crown of Thorns* (1987), a biography of King Boris III, was well received in Bulgaria and abroad. Virtually all international studies on Bulgarian history in the1930s and 1940s refer to it. Other books by Groueff were published in Bulgaria after the Changes (Groueff 2002).

 Like Groueff, *Stephen Constant* (Stojan-Konstantin Danev 1933) was an emigrant whose work *Foxy Ferdinand, 1861–1948, Tsar of Bulgaria* (1980) first appeared not only in English, but under English version of the author's name. He was an English journalist of Bulgarian origin, born in Sofia. Both Groueff and Constant wrote in Bulgarian and in English for an international audience. Their significant authority and popularity is chiefly due to the historical subject matter, censored in Bulgaria before the Changes, but also to their use of sources, unknown to the general public and scholars alike, their émigré status, and the international success of their work.

 Georgi Markov (1929–1978) is the most well-known and probably the most typical political emigrant from the second wave. The reception of his works has not yet been fully analyzed. Before 1969, Markov was a well-known writer who was connected in a sense to the communist elite. Later he was sentenced in absentia to six years imprisonment and anathematized by state propaganda. His books were withdrawn from public libraries, yet gained a new popularity, reinforced by his famous broadcasts for *BBC*, *Deutsche Welle* and *Radio Free Europe*. Published in printed form outside Bulgaria, his broadcasts became even more popular. After the Changes they were reprinted in new editions in Bulgaria. His few literary works were translated and so well received by readers, the media, and the critics, that few people noticed (or dared to mention) Markov's sincerely declared fidelity to communism and insistence on the need to purify communism from the distortions caused by particular rulers.

Several books about Georgi Markov appeared in Bulgaria in the years after the fall of the Berlin Wall. They varied greatly in quality and intention. All of them focused on Markov's assassination and did not scrutinize his literary work. *Ubijte Skitnik* (*Kill the Wanderer*, 2005) by Christo Christov stands out among them. Christov is also author of *Dăržavna sigurnost sreshtu bălgarskata emigracija* (*State Security against Bulgarian Emigration*, 2000). The great interest in Markov was undeniably politically motivated and produced numerous biographies and memoirs. Many of the authors of Markov's generation declared they were his friends. There were also some attempts to delve into his private life, which is not so typical for the Bulgarian context.

Vladimir Kostov (1932), who also pretended to be the target of assassination plans, published a book about Markov's murder – *Bălgarskijat chadăr* (*The Bulgarian Umbrella*, 1990), returned to Bulgaria and became again one of the leading journalists in Bulgaria, where he continued to publish. His anti-communism was more problematic. It transpired that he was member of the Bulgarian secret services; and he gradually re-joined his former friends from communist circles. This kind of development always drastically changes not only the author's image, but his reading public as well.

Rumiana Uzunova (1936–1995), a literary critic (Uzunova 1980), who emigrated in 1980, was an active journalist and critic. She took part in many dissident activities, and also returned to Bulgaria for a short period after 1989. A crime novel with autobiographical elements written years ago by Uzunova was published posthumously (Uzunova, 2007). The book was prominently reviewed but cannot claim popularity.

After the Changes emigrants became fashionable. They were positively presented in the media and their books were (re)published in Bulgaria. Some books became popular despite media criticisms and even accusations of antisemitism. One representative figure was *Nikola M. Nikolov* (1920–1997), author of *Svetovnata konspiracija* (*World Conspiracy*, 1990)[2]. Nikolov's case was only one extreme manifestation of the attitude of established institutions toward returning emigrants and their work. Here again different factors were at play. Some themes, problems, viewpoints and social gestures are still forbidden fruits and arouse curiosity despite rejection by official reviews. Information on such books spreads by word of mouth.

Dimiter Inkiov (1932–2006) was one of the most successful Bulgarian authors with a considerable international success. In Bulgaria he worked as a journalist, trying his hand at different genres (poetry, drama, science fiction). As emigrant in Germany he gained a reputation with the Bulgarian public, mainly *Radio Free Europe* listeners, with feuilletons and comic short stories, broadcasted under his pen name Velko Verin. In Germany he became a successful author of about one hundred children's books, many of them translated into other languages and used in schools. But as an author of feuilletons, the emigrant Inkiov (Verin) was totally immersed in the Bulgarian social environment, problems, and traditions. As a writer for children, he referred to other social environments, was engaged in other traditions and followed other patterns. After the Changes, Inkiov was extensively published in Bulgaria and enjoyed broad attention. There are numerous translations of his children's books. A good many readers remembered his satirical works from the Cold War time and were happy to have them collected in books (Inkiov 1992, 2003, 2004).

Atanas Slavov (1930) is another prolific emigrant author of poems, fiction, memoirs, journalism, scholarship, criticism, and translations in both Bulgarian and English. In many of these genres he was an established author even before leaving the country for the United States in 1975–1976. While abroad he published in English and Bulgarian. More than other émigré writers, he successfully integrates Bulgarian traditions with the traditions he acquired in a foreign culture. This synthesis is evident even in his early texts, although his work as a whole takes a critical attitude towards borrowed elements. Some of his studies were first published in Polish, but he is firmly rooted in Bulgarian culture. He was one of the few emigrants to return after the Changes. In the past decade he offered new editions of his previous publications and old manuscripts as well as new work (Slavov 1998, 2005b, 2007). Excluding some political figures, Slavov is one of the few contemporary Bulgarian authors who has recently been publishing his selected works in several volumes (Slavov 2005a). Very few other writers of his generation have their own web site.

Tsvetan Marangozov (1933) followed a different path. He emigrated in 1960 after the publication of his novel *Bezličnijat* (*Non-persona*, 1959, 2003)[3]. In Germany Marangozov built a successful career as a screenwriter, producer, and composer, and then after the Changes he also published poetry, drama, and essays in Bulgarian. He became very popular almost immediately among certain intellectuals who published a collection of critical essays on his work (Konstantinova 2002). Marangozov's approach to Bulgarian and foreign traditions is too complex to be summarized in a few sentences. As a poet and playwright Marangozov seeks contact mainly with his Bulgarian public. While in Germany he did not attempt to emphasize the so-called Bulgarian 'exoticism'.

Probably most renowned abroad are two Bulgarians who both left the country in the 1960s.

Tzvetan Todorov (1939) is a well-known Franco-Bulgarian philosopher with scientific work in the fields of literary theory, thought and culture theory. It was in the beginning of 1980's that his work reached Bulgaria. After the Changes his work was published in Bulgarian and received academic acclaim (e.g. Atanasov 2001). Initially alienated from Bulgaria and the Bulgarian language, after 1989 he has published semi-biographical work and studies on the state of emigration, communist and Nazi concentration camps and the memory of the victims of those regimes (Todorov 1989, 1999, 2003).

Like Todorov, *Julia Kristeva* (1941) is primarily known for her scholarly contribution on semiotics, psycho-analysis and gender studies. After the Changes she wrote semi-autobiographical novels portraying emigration and Bulgaria under communism and in transition (Kristeva 1990, 1994, 2006).

In the 1970s the political situation led to a new group of emigrants, who emigrated because they were repressed, tried, sentenced, and jailed. One of them, *Lubomir Kanov* (1944) was arrested in 1977, imprisoned, and migrated to Canada in 1984 after his release. He became a psychiatrist in New York. After the Changes he visited Bulgaria several times and published books written in Bulgarian for a Bulgarian audience. One critic wrote of him:

> Единствената книга на К., излязла досега, сборникът разкази „Човекът куковица" (1991)... не би могла да се нарече „емигрантска", защото е инспирирана, а и създадена в българската обществена и културна ситуация на 70-те и 80-те години. Част от разказите са замислени, докато К. е в затвора.
>
> (K's only published work is his collection of short stories *The Cuckoo Man* [1991]... It cannot be labeled "emigrant" because it is inspired by and created in the Bulgarian cultural and social environment of the 1970s and 1980s. Some of these short stories were drafted when K. was in prison.) (Vatova, 1994: 163)

Dimitar Bočev (1944) left Bulgaria in 1972 for Germany. He had some background as a writer and started to work for *Radio Free Europe*. After the Changes he wrote books in Bulgarian for a Bulgarian readership, which refer to events in Bulgaria and are not without some autobiographical elements. Bočev, Kanov and probably Marangozov can be best described as *Bulgarian writers living abroad.*

Many other authors living abroad appeared after the Changes. It is not enough to call them emigrants despite the fact that some of them applied for this status in the early 1990s. Some of them write in Bulgarian, some do not write in Bulgarian but nevertheless target the Bulgarian public.

A compendium of authors living abroad who write in Bulgarian and follow some of the Bulgarian traditions, deliberately trying to reinstate themselves, could possibly begin with *Alexander Andreev* (1956), who made his debut in Bulgaria, went to work for *Deutsche Welle* in Cologne, but published fiction and translations mainly in Bulgarian. His novel *Novi stepeni na svoboda* (*New Degrees of Freedom,* 1999) represents a radical parody of the spy novels typical of Bogomil Rajnov. A year before that, Andreev published *Zagovorăt na špionite* (*The Conspiracy of the Spies,* 1998), a nonfiction work.

Similarly, *Vladislav Todorov* (1956) became a university lecturer in the United States in the 1990s. In addition to scholarly work in Bulgarian and English, he published the novel *Zift* (*'Asphalt'*, 2006), which parodies typical patterns of crime writing, situated in 1950s Bulgaria. In a similar vein are writers such as Vladimir Levčev, Tzveta Sofronieva, Milena Fučedžieva, and Nikita Nankov, living abroad and writing in Bulgarian and other languages.

Zlatko Enev (1961) occupies a special place among such writers. Located in Berlin he maintains an interesting online periodical, *Liberal Review* (www.librev.com), aimed at a Bulgarian public and another, *Ecrivains de Bulgarie* (http://litbg.free.fr) in cooperation with the eminent French translator Marie Vrinat, which targets an international audience. He writes mainly fantasy in Bulgarian. This genre does not have a long tradition in Bulgarian literature so it is difficult to say whether he is following Bulgarian tradition. Ivan Kuslev, a sculptor in Holland using the penname Barry Cussel, works in a similar fashion.

Recently *Zachari* (*Zack*) *Karabashliev* (1968) caught the attention of the public. He lives in the United States where he writes plays. One of his plays was staged in Los Angeles and another received an award in Bulgaria. His novel *18 % sivo* (*18 % grey*, 2008) was one of the literary events of the year. This autobiographical work, describing the life of an emigrant, was written in Bulgarian, published in Bulgaria, and, according to some journalists, successfully employs the model of *On the Road* by Jack Kerouac.

Even more closely related to new developments in Bulgarian literature are *Alek Popov* (1966), *Viktor Paskov* (1949–2009) and *Albena Stambolova*, authors who after some time spent abroad have returned as Bulgarian authors in Bulgaria.

Political reasons for leaving Bulgaria virtually disappeared after the Changes, although there were probably some attempts to use such arguments on the grounds of ethnic, religious, or gender discrimination. One such case was *Nikolaj Atanasov* who, after leaving the county, published a collection of verses *Organični formi* (*Organic Forms*, 2007) in Bulgaria, which received the attention of the critics:

Ако събитие е онова, което не̃ се побира в изработените по един или друг начин хоризонти, то за мен през 2007 това беше стихосбирката на Николай Атанасов "Органични форми". Съкрушителната й автобиографичност е съчетана с подривна литературност – опит да се излезе в гръб на традицията, да се извади наяве един алтернативен литературен канон на потиснатото различие по линията Лилиев-Вутимски-Георги Мицков. Писана извън България на което вероятно се дължи част от свободата й, тя е изненадващо своевременна – би било полезно, да речем, четенето й в бъкащото от насилие българско училище.

(If an event is what transcends already formed horizons of expectation, for me, in 2007, this was Nikolaj Atanasov's poetry collection *Organic Forms*. Its crushing autobiographical mode is combined with a subversive literary approach – an attempt to attack tradition from behind, to bring to light an alternative literary canon of oppressed divergence along the lines of Liliev - Vutimski – Georgy Mitskov. Written abroad, which at least partly explains its freedom of expression, at the same time it strikes with its actuality here. This book should be read in the constrained atmosphere of Bulgarian schools).[4]

At the other end of the spectrum are authors who live abroad, write in another language, and are subsequently translated into Bulgarian. The most renowned names are Dimitré Dinew and Iliya Troyanov. Very different in style and approach, they have successfully reached Bulgarian readers as writers in German.

Dimitré Dinev (1968) is an Austrian author of Bulgarian origin who settled in Vienna in 1990. Although his reasons for emigrating are not so transparent, in some interviews he has mentioned political motives. He is the author of several books that were originally published in German and several dramatic works. His novel *Engelszungen* (2006) was published in Bulgarian in the same year, but Dinew's name became better known when his play *Koža i nebe* (*Haut und Himmel*) won the important *Askeer* prize in 2007. His award provoked considerable public debate on the question of whether a text written in German by an author who is an Austrian citizen should be awarded a Bulgarian literary prize. The well-known dramatist Konstantin Iliev, also nominated for the award, withdrew his play *Beethoven 21* from the competition.

Less deliberately provocative is Iliya Troyanov (1965) who also publishes in German and is translated into English and other languages. His novel *Die Welt ist gross und Rettung lauert überall* (1994) has seen two editions in Bulgarian translation and enjoys flattering reviews. Even more popular is the film version (2008, director Stefan Komandarev), which has been shortlisted for the 2010 Oscar nomination. Along with the many positive reviews, there are a few caustic remarks to be found in Internet forums, which raise the fact that Troyanov is a convert to Islam.

The reception of the film *Baklava,* or, more precisely its trailer, caused quite a stir.[5] Directed by *Alexo Petrov*, a young Bulgarian who recently relocated to Canada, the film was first screened on September 3, 2007 at the Varna Film festival and in Sofia. The scandal erupted at the beginning of 2008 when official institutions in Bulgaria reacted to the scenes of violence and sex in trailers uploaded onto the Internet. The real problem was not the sex and violence but the portrayal of everyday reality in a Bulgarian orphanage. Legal proceedings brought charges for distribution of pornography and employing persons under the age of 16 without the necessary permission. This case is significant for the recurrence of official suspicion with regard to critical view-points about Bulgaria, particularly those emanating from emigrants

In conclusion let us summarize the observations, bearing in mind their preliminary character. Every work of art needs an element that attracts public attention. One such element is the plight of exile; but although interesting, this is not always sufficient, and its efficiency decreases over time.

In addition to the influence of official propaganda and counter-propaganda, the reception of émigré literature is governed by at least two factors. On the one hand, such works focus attention on and gain authority from an emigrant's misfortune and the recognition of his or her work abroad. That said, not all emigrants succeed in problematizing the emigrant's existence but some (Kristeva, Todorov, Bočev, Karabashliev, to name a few) show greater affinity for this kind of reflection.

On the other hand, apart from envy and frustration, there is always some skepticism (not always groundless) toward émigré writings. Some émigré literature, whatever the case may be, corresponds to a kind of yesterday, a past situation that is not fully identical with the present, if not from a political point of view then at least from a cultural perspective. This is not a problem in the case of memoirs or historical texts (even those dealing with the recent past), but poses difficulties when ideas from yesterday are applied to today with the declared aim of pronouncing truth about the present. This truth sometimes appears to be quite 'Westernized', close to a stereotypical Western image of (communist) Eastern Europe.

The aspirations for *high* literature and the universal values of some of the emigrants from the first wave are not frequently suitable for the current (post-modern) situation. This is why in recent years one can note a diversity of approaches by emigrant authors aiming at specific segments of readers. This naturally generates a heterogeneous array of reactions, which is actually the normal reception for all literature.

Notes

[1] Atanas Dalčev's biography is extremely interesting. He was born in Thessalonica (1904) in Greece. His father was briefly a member of the Ottoman Parliament. When he was ten years old he came to live in Bulgaria, but later lived for a short period in Turkey. In his writing one sees influences of France where he lived between 1928–1929 and 1936–1937. He is one of the most renowned Bulgarian poets but has also translated poetry from Russian, French, Spanish etc. He died in 1978.

[2] Online biographies of Nikola M. Nikolov note: Born in 1920 in Vidin, was an officer of the tsar in the World War II, political prisoner after 1944, emigrated in 1969 to the US. His books were published in many languages. He died in 1997 under mysterious circumstances.

[3] After the Changes the novels was published in its original form without the imposed censorship (1993a).

[4] Quote from http://www.slovo.bg/showwork.php3?AuID=38&WorkID=16629&Level=1. This site presents Atanasov as: "Nikolay Atanasov received several national awards for literature: among them also the prestigious *South Spring* for the Best Book for 1999. He was also compiler of the first in its genre, a study of the roots of Bulgarian gay culture, published in a special issue of *Literaturen vestnik* (No.19, 2000)".

[5] The official site of the film is http://baklava-themovie.com. The official blog site: http://b-a-k-l-a-v-a.blogspot.com. There are also numerous comments in the media and elsewhere on the Internet.

Bibliography

Andreev, Aleksandar. 1999. *Novi spomeni na svoboda*. Sofia: Atlantis KL.

Atanasov, Stojan (ed.) 2001. *Tzvetan Todorov – podvižnata misăl*. Sofia: Univ. izd. Sv. Kliment Ohridski.

Atanasov, Nikolaj. 2007. *Organični formi*. Sofia: Altera.

Christov, Christo. 2000. *Dăržavna sigurnost sreštu bălgarskata emigracija*. Sofia: Ivan Vazov.

— 2005. *Ubijte Skitnik*. Sofia: Siela.

Constant, Stephen. 1980. *Foxy Ferdinand: tsar of Bulgaria*. New York/London/Toronto: Franklin Watts.

Dinev, Dimitré. 2003. *Engelszungen*. Wien: Deuticke (Angelski ezici. Sofia: Riva, 2006).

— 2006. *Haut und Himmel*. Wien: Rabenhof. (Koža i nebe, 2007).

Groueff, Stephen. 1991. *Crown of Thorns* (*Korona ot trăni*). Sofia: Bălgarski Pisatel.

— 2002. *Mojata odiseja*. Sofia: Obsidian.

Inkiov, Dimităr. 1992. *Vesela nedelja*. Sofia: Univ. izd. Sv. Konstantin Ohridski.

— 2003. *Botuš Kašev i drugite*. Sofia: 5 zvezdi.

— 2004. *Botuš Kašev i novoto vreme*. Sofia: 5 zvezdi.

Kanov, Lubomir. 1991. *Čovekăt kukuvica*. Sofia: Petrinov.

Karabelova, Magda (ed.) 1996. *Izgnaničestvo. Drama i motivacija*. Sofia: Akad. Izd. Prof. M.Drinov.

Karabashev, Zachari (Zach). 2009. *18 % sivo*. Sofia

Konstantinova, Elka & Marieta Ivanova – Girginova (eds). 2002. *Bitie i identičnost. Tzvetan Marangozov – poetăt, pisteljat*. Sofia: izd. Centăr Bpjan Penev.

Kristeva, Julia. 1991a. *Etrangers á nous-mêmes*. Paris: Flammarion.

— 1991b. *Le vieil home et les loups*. Paris: Fayard.

— 1996. *Possessions*. Paris: Fayard.

— 2004. *Meurtre á Byzans*. Paris: Livre de Poche.

Marangozov, Tzvetan. 1993. *Bezličnijat*. 2 izd. Sofia: Bălgarski pisatel. *Bezličnijat*. Originalăt. Sofia: Izdatelsko atelie Ab.

Ognjanov, Christo. 1992. *Aziski soneti* (tr. Inge Ognyanova). Sofia: Edem 21.

— 1995. *Bălgarski istoričeski kalendar*. Sofia: izd. avt.

Popov, Stefan. 1938. *Planini i hora*. Sofia

— 1992. *Bezsănici*. Sofia: Letopisi.

— 1994. *Bălgarskata ideja*. Sofia: Letopisi.

— 1999. *Ideiite za Evropa prez vekovete*. Sofia: Juliana – M, Lik.

Slavov, Atanas. 2005a. *Izbrani sačinenija*. vols. 1–4. Jambol: Ja.

— 2005b. *Noštite na Trentăn: Karnavalno šestvie na Al Santana*. The complete version. Sofia: Iztok – Zapad.

Šiškova, Magdalena et al. (eds.). 1994 *Rečnik na nova bălgarska literatura 1878– 1992*. Sofia: Hemus.

Todorov, Tzvetan. 1989. *Nous et les autres*. Paris: Seuil.

— 1996. *L'homme depaysé*. Paris: Seuil.

— 1998a. *Život s drugite*. Sofia: Nauka i Izkustvo.

— 1998b. *Na čužda zemja*. Sofia: Otvoreno obštestvo.

— 2000. *Mémoire du mal, tentation du bien*. Paris: Robert Laffont.

— 2001. *Pamet za zloto, izkušenie za dobroto*. Sofia: IK Lik.

Troyanov, Iliya. 1994. *Die Welt ist gross und Rettung lauert überall*. Munich: Hanser Verlag.

— 1997 (2007). *Svetăt e goljam i spasenie debne otvsjakăde*. Sofia: Siela.

Uzunova, Rumjana. 1980. *Pavel Vežinov. Kritičeski očerk*. Sofia: Bălgarski pisatel.

— 2000. *Ubijstvo v stil rokoko*. Sofia: Siela.

Vatova, Penka. 1994. 'Ljubomir Kanov' in Šiškova Magdalena et al.(eds.). *Rečnik po nova bălgarska literatura*. Sofia: Hemus: 162–163.

The *Other* Road.
On the Bulgarian Topos in the Work of Three Writers Awarded the Adelbert von Chamisso Prize

Penka Angelova

Abstract: This paper considers the contribution to world literature of three Bulgarian writers living abroad. Their work introduces certain Bulgarian topoi as new crossing ground for global understanding while at the same time representing new traditions for Bulgarian literature.
Keywords: gaze from outside, coping with the past, culture memory, rapprochement of mental worlds.

A *Frankfurter Allgemeine* reporter asked me how Bulgaria would enter the European Union with authors no one knows about. The authors with whom the European reader associates Bulgaria are by no means those considered national authors in Bulgaria according to the canon. In the last few years interest in Bulgaria has certainly increased considerably throughout Western Europe and a couple of modern Bulgarian authors have been translated. Art is the natural way to know and 'bring cultures closer'. And yet translation is a difficult and hazardous challenge, particularly where 'small languages' and lesser known cultures are concerned, where cultural background is hard to translate or requires additional explanations.

One of the roads to world literature passes through the German language, as was the case with some Norwegian authors at the beginning of the last century. This is the 'other' and somehow more direct road to world literature. Therefore I will focus here on three authors of Bulgarian origin who write in German and have already been recognized not only by the German reading public but have adequate recognition in Bulgaria as well: Iliya Troyanov, Dimitré Dinev and Tzveta Sofronieva. They are the authors of a considerably wide spectrum of genres – novels, short and long stories, non-fiction, poetry, and drama. Therefore within this brief framework, I will consider only those aspects of their art which in my opinion have made them typical 'go-betweens' and bearers of a certain Bulgarian topos.

I will start with the fact that the topos 'Bulgaria as a fatherland' was introduced into German-language literature during the 1970s by Elias Canetti in his biographical book *Die gerettete Zunge* (*The Tongue Set Free*, 1977). Naturally, there had been material written on Bulgaria before, but it was always from an external vantage point, from the view point of a foreigner with a different cultural and historical background, a person confronting otherness, seeking and presenting proof or disproof of his own expectations and for whom a visit or sojourn in that region was related to the exotics or to literary topoi. "Everything I experienced later, I had already experienced before in Ruschuk".[1] This is the point of a story teller, analyzing experience in the context of childhood and looking for relationships and continuities between places and events, starting with his childhood adventures in the town on the Danube.

Iliya Troyanov, who can certainly be characterized with the title of his own book *Der Weltensammler* (*The Collector of Worlds*, 2006), having many years' experience of three continents and numerous international awards and translations into foreign languages, left his country like Canetti at the age of six, but has preserved unambiguous engagement with Bulgaria, full of responsibility and pain. There are four books in which he incorporates the 'Bulgarian topos': *Die Welt ist gross und Rettung lauert überall* (*The World is Big and Salvation Lurks Around the Corner*, 1996), *Hundezeiten* (*Dog Days*, 2008), *Die fingierte Revolution. Bulgarien, eine exemplarische Geschichte* (*The Made-Up Revolution. Bulgaria. An Exemplary Story*, 2006) and *Der entfesselte Globus* (*The Unchained Globe*, 2008). And whereas the novel *Die Welt ist gross...* was published in Bulgarian as long ago as 1998, though in a limited print run and with rather poor distribution, *Кучешки времена* (*Hundezeiten*)[2] had to wait nearly ten years to be published in its new version as *Фиктивната революция* (*Die fingierte Revolution*). No Bulgarian publisher could be found at that time who would publish the book, while the translator, whom Iliya Troyanov's German publisher engaged, asked the author with native black-eyed naïveté: "How could you write so about Bulgaria?" *For Bulgaria – either good or nothing at all*, especially in front of 'foreigners'. It is a saying each child memorizes in its early years along with the obligation to be proud of being Bulgarian, because Bulgarian identity does not allow for any other feelings but pride.

In Bulgaria *Фиктивната революция* (*Die fingierte Revolution*) is being read as history and it is to Iliya Troyanov's credit that the story is preserved in the memory culture – with arrogant Todor Živkov[3] citations and Bulgarian media opportunism. In Germany the book leaves an impression of surrealistic literature – the same arrogant citations and opportunistic behavior are seen as literary methods: the foreign reader would hardly imagine it is not simply fiction or the author's sense of humor. A colleague of mine, a professor at a (West) German university was, for example, convinced of Iliya Troyanov's talent for hyperbole – a literary method in German-language literature of the last few decades. Troyanov himself defines his book as non-fiction.

Iliya Troyanov's *Hundezeiten* is a work of non-fiction documenting the last half century through observations and interviews with successful and unsuccessful politicians, with workers and country dwellers, as well as with victims who even nowadays are 'criminalized' by Bulgarian politics without access to the political stage and to decision-making institutions and councils, for fear they might disclose the on-going crimes of the true criminals. Despite its documentary nature, the book displays the strict literary structure typical of Troyanov, passing through all of society's layers and thus creating the panorama of a confused population left at the mercy of yesterday's dictators and today's oligarchs. The open framework structure beginning with the 'swan's song' of the former totalitarian 'chieftain' anticipates the impending story and structurally introduces the government conspiracy.

This is a book about Bulgaria and Bulgarian political life over the last five decades, written in the best literary tradition and with the conceptual apparatus of German anti-totalitarian – i.e. anti-Nazi and anti-Communist – thinking; in the tradition set up by philosophers like Hannah Arendt and Adorno, introduced into the educational system of German schools and universities, the language that formed German democracy. There are two specific concepts in that language that shape attitudes to the past which should find adequate translations into other languages as well, because there is no country where pride in the past is not connected with shameful, criminal periods in its history.

However, considerations and reactions in this respect are rather scanty in nationalist discourses.

These are the concepts of coping with the past and the opposition *perpetrator–victim*. In the German tradition *Vergangenheitsbewältigung* is crucial in making sense of and handling the past. This crucial 'making sense' shapes a nation's culture of memory. Iliya Troyanov's book is an attempt and an appeal to such a redefinition of the manipulated and hidden myths in present day Bulgaria. There is no opposition *perpetrator–victim* in the Bulgarian language; the usual opposition is *criminal–victim* and it creates an unsurpassable abyss between the two concepts. The fact that no such opposition occurs in the Bulgarian language does not mean it does not exist; it only means that officially the situation is being manipulated and hidden – a fact by virtue of which the perpetrators of Communist times were able to initiate and build up mafias during the so-called 'façade' democracy period. Victims remained silent/unseen. In order to make sense of the past, a new conceptual system should be set up, the new world has to find its own new language.

Iliya Troyanov's "gaze from outside" rearranges and takes out the information from the "inside", from the "Augean stables of post-Communist Bulgarian reality" (Milen Radev)[4], in the comfort of whose warmth a whole society is still ruminating on the old myths, still considering itself a victim and demanding no responsibility from the actors/perpetrators.

In his collection of essays *Der entfesselte Globus* (2008) Troyanov places the 'experience' of post-totalitarian Bulgaria in the post-colonial discourse of the freed, unshackled, breaking through and uncontrolled forces of terror the world over.

With his novels and his film[5] about Bulgaria Iliya Troyanov reasserts his responsibility as an artist and his civil conscience as citizen of the world and writer. The writer's profession was defined in the same way by Elias Canetti: "If words can achieve so much, why shouldn't they also prevent? No wonder persons handling words better than others, rely more on the power of words."[6]

It is my sincere hope that this book will bring a fresh current into the culture of memory in Bulgaria, that it will provoke interest in the near past, in its perpetrators and victims. Because truth can be documented and should be collected from living witnesses. The rest is mythology.

Dimitré Dinev left Bulgaria at the age of twenty, remaining homeless for some time and experiencing the troubles of life in migration. In an interview he describes how another homeless man in his rambling years asked him about the place he came from and he decided to answer with a question, describing the boundaries of the Danube, the Black Sea, Greece and Turkey. "Well, there's nothing there", replied the homeless man. It is that 'nothing' that has become a topos in Dinev's literary works. So far he has published two collections of short stories and a novel.[7] The themes in his short stories and his novel may be specified as the typical immigrant literature that enjoy great success in the German-speaking countries. The novel *Engelszungen* (*Angels speaking in Tongues*, 2003) was introduced onto some school curricula in Vienna. It is in this sense that Dinev presents in his works the 'otherness', the Balkan otherness of unknown neighbors.

I read the novel with great interest, 'in one breath', as far as one could say that for a novel saga of six hundred pages. But the tension is maintained and makes you keep reading and following the plot: the fate of two young men of a lost Bulgarian generation, seeking their luck right after the crucial turn in 1989 in Vienna – historically the nearest harbor of Bulgarian refugees.

But this is also a novel *of* society and *about* society: a novel presenting two family sagas from the beginning to the end of the twentieth century – our short and yet long enough century full of crimes against mankind. The novel depicts both the history and the psychology of the twentieth-century Bulgarian. The novel is written in German and is destined for German-language readers matching both the style and the themes of the German-language novel or rather the Austrian novel around the millennium. Here, however, we meet an author who represents a completely new tradition and new generation in Bulgarian literature. For the Bulgarian reader this is the first novel within decades to present an unbelievable sweep of the historical panorama of several generations. Neither the Soldier's Uprising, nor Stambolijski's[8] regime are forgotten here, nor the Bulgarian pseudo-revolutions and liberations. For the first time a panoramic novel does not take place against the background of idyllic country life, but is set in a purely urban environment, unfolding in one of the big towns in Bulgaria with a pronounced urban tradition. Fortunately the novel is not developed against the background of an ethnically controversial population – for some time a literary fashion in a Bulgaria trying to integrate minorities by means of novel trilogies. Therefore the novel in a sense is a novelty in the Bulgarian literary tradition, too.

There is a Balkan magical realism here: neither adapted, nor artificial but somehow pure Bulgarian naturalism; but outside Bulgaria it has been received as something funny and curious: all this godlessness, these maledictions and superstition. "Religion was forbidden, Vanga[9] was not." And a rigid faith in the magic power of words. The spirit of a late priest appears here who disturbed the gypsies that settled down in his home, until he found his axe; roaming clairvoyants and psychics reading coffee-cups, palms and other limbs, miracle workers, sorcerers, healers – all of them pieces of the puzzle in a dearly familiar picture. And suddenly, in a single sweep, a new time dimension occurs, a black hole in time that sucks us in and hurls us into the realms of Francis of Assisi and Grigorij Rasputin: the new post-Communist saint is the former Communist malefactor and criminal killer, his wife's lover's dried-up tongue hanging around his neck. Isn't this a new kind of Christian resignation – that those people outside the law would finally be brought before the law of their own conscience? Or hope in a world bereft of any transcendence and human values that there is after all justice beyond conscience? In the vacuum of morality and human values hanging like a black sky over all our society, a little ray of hope twinkles, but also stronger skepticism as to the moral territory of the devil's circle: do we need the saints who used to be the cause of our misery, and who now have to perform magic to heal us?

Similarly crucial in this perspective is the parody of the liberator myth, of the eternal Bulgarian hope for help from abroad: the meeting of the two protagonists at the tombstone of Milo the Serb, who perched on his tombstone with mobile phone in hand turns into a ministering angel and a guardian angel of the refugees bereaved of any hope. "The Serbs cannot even help themselves and we are expecting help from a dead Serb."

This is in fact an extraordinary, polyvalent humor built from mysterious irony and vital cynicism. It is not surprising that the novel provoked great positive reaction in the German-language community; it is read with great empathy by many migrants. It is interesting and no less readable for the Bulgarian public, too, and for the Bulgarian literary tradition, which following Elias Canetti, opens up our route to world literature.

Tzveta Sofronieva arrived in Germany at the age of twenty-eight after having lived in the USA and Canada. She has settled down at present in Berlin, writing poetry, essays and prose in Bulgarian, English and German. Of the three authors analyzed here, Sofronieva is perhaps the least German one, fully aware of her Bulgarian literary roots; she has lots of 'soil' glued to the soles of her shoes that later has taken over specks of dust from the English-language world. Sofronieva, who studied physics and has retained a strong interest in quantum mechanics, and who has done research on science and philosophy, rationalizes her relationship to earth in an unambiguously philosophical and theoretical manner, reflecting on linguistic barriers and looking for bridges and meeting places between them. She links in a unique way the mythological thinking of Eastern orthodox religion with the rationality of the Enlightenment by blending Mythos and Logos in her work.

My attention in the present study is focused on the Bulgarian topos in German-language texts and therefore I will be analyzing Tzveta Sofronieva's texts *Trost* (Consolation, 2005) and *Andere (W)orte (M)other words,* 2006). The essay *Andere (W)orte* is directly associated with *Verbotene worte* (*Forbidden words*), the international writers' network initiated by Tzveta Sofronieva in the mid-nineties that investigates linguistic memory and intercultural misunderstanding. Writing produced under the auspices of this network has been presented in a digital anthology on *Kakanien,* a website published by the University of Vienna,[10] and in the trilingual electronic literary journal *Transcript*, which is published by the University of Aberystwyth.[11] With this initiative inspired by her essays *Andere (W)orte* and *Gefangen im Light oder die Sprache als verbotene Heimat* (*Caught in the Light or Language as a Forbidden Homeland,* 2006), Tzveta Sofronieva began a conversation on communication between cultures that proved to be painfully topical. Numerous symposia, readings and discussions took place with authors from California to Japan and from New Zealand to Sweden and most of all from Central Europe.

It is a common truth that word-for-word translation is no good. But whenever the author who writes in a certain language is confronted not only with the untranslatability but the impossibility of bringing up certain words, with their political and historical burden, the problem turns existential. Every author writing in a foreign language faces the same problem. It is an intercultural problem that with increasing global mobility has become even more current. Tzveta Sofronieva reflects and writes on this issue, she is looking for "traces in the words" left behind by previous usages. Perhaps the basic problem in these texts is best specified by the protagonist of the short story *Trost* - Anani: "After all you don't use words the same way they were used by those German speaking men – Marx, Freud and Hitler" (p.80).[12]

This is a problem concerning both the culture of memory and attitudes towards it, towards political correctness and political culture, and not in the least historiography and content or pedagogical methods. In this context, Tzveta Sofronieva moves along the border, along the two language boundaries, searching for a place for her words. How can two languages, developed on two contradictory national myths, on two contradictory complexes – the complex of the 'perpetrators' guilt and the complex of the 'victims' of every kind of conspiracy – find a common language? How can Protestant ethics and Eastern orthodoxy be reconciled? "The boundaries of my language are the boundaries of my world", says Ludwig Wittgenstein. Bulgarian language boundaries are traditionally hard and impermeable, they are canonized with the imminent orthodox loyalty to words. The stereotypes formed up back in childhood for 'the sacred language of my fathers' and the sacred land, for which so much blood had been shed and in the indisputable WE that is ever present in all historical writings: we in the first, second, third Bulgarian kingdoms, we in the wars etc. Nobody in Germany considers the German language sacred, and the reference to 'Blut und Boden' is completely clear and painfully associated with the notorious myths of the Third Reich. Every child knows this! The 'Heimat – Homeland' is also associated in educated German circles with the 'Heimatliteratur' of the inter-war period or with the films of the 1950s, with the novels engaged with a countryside idyll that maintained the myth of the sound German spirit. And if sociology has long ago found that the term nation has no denomination except in the pre-election speeches of politicians, that society consists of many societies or is "people in configurations" (Norbert Ellias) – this is much more accepted in the German language where the terms 'nation' and 'national' are rarely used and are rather 'historicized'.

There are no 'forbidden' words in that sense in the Bulgarian language, one can speak freely and at ease with a mixture of centuries old nationalism and with a communist vocabulary as well as a mixture of fascist and racist terminology, depending on one's habits, on one's feelings as a free person in a postmodern dimension in which the period from the seventh till the twenty-first century is somehow a permanent present, nourished by the 'glorious past' distributed between the subjects WE, YOU and THEY. And the most recent past is pushed out of the collective consciousness in the way described by Sigmund Freud. Typical for the Bulgarian language is the pathos of belonging, inculcated since elementary school. Typical for the German language is the anti-pathos of playfulness.

Yet there is a common denominator between the two cultures and the two languages: the unique manner in which they react to evil and to victims respectively. The German language cannot accept the name 'concentration camp' in the meaning of communist camps, it cannot allow the comparison between Communist and National-Socialist evil. The Bulgarian language does not accept that another nation can suffer more than the Bulgarian nation, and does not allow any outside viewpoint. Memory culture in Bulgaria is rationalized mainly in university communities and the young generations are a good example of the social amnesia of the recent past. In the German language the 'forbidden words' have passed through the purgatory of sixty years of rationalizing the language of the Third Reich and the language of the 'victorious' socialism. No purgatory of this kind has yet occurred in the Bulgarian language. It has been rationalized only by individual authors but has not been accorded any social or educational significance.

This is the difficult dilemma confronted by the protagonist of *Trost,* as well as by the author of *Andere (W)orte.* Sofronieva is interested in the literary use of these loaded and abused German words. "I still want to know whether one uses other words in German for feelings that I refer to using words that are troubled in German – or do people no longer have these feelings? And if people don't have them anymore, has something else grown in their place or are they gone completely and forever?" (Andere (W)orte, 2007). She is, however, fully aware of 'the purgatory' these words have gone through.

Trost is a short story in two parts. The plot starts on the western Bulgarian border. The first part is entitled *Siebzehn Quelen, siebzehn Kriege* (*Seventeen springs, seventeen wars*) – a spring for each war – and covers almost a century; this is the life of Anani, the founder of the family, who never managed to return to his birth place.

> Anani's soul disappeared into history, a history no one wanted to talk about, because it had followed a course that was politically incorrect. Anani's soul never made itself felt. A century had probably been long enough for it. (p.77)

The second part, *Das Rivier der Schicksalsgöttin* (*The territory of the Goddess of Fate*), covers a couple of days in the life of Anani's granddaughter Anaani who lives and works at a European institution in Germany and tries to rationalize the borders and bridges between languages and her place in those bordering situations. And who lives up her grandfather's rebirth into a slug, a shell-less snail[13] for whom she fails to take responsibility, but she assumes responsibility for the guilt. In the second part devoted to Ananke, the goddess of fate, the author reveals in both a rational and mystical manner the contact zone of the two languages and the two manners of thinking, the two types of literary approach: the devotion to Bulgarian literature and language, and the civil urban territory of German literature. Scientific knowledge of physics and quantum mechanics, *yin* and *yang*, in the space between antique myth and cloning, all in emotional images, depict in this short story the "soul of memory", of "forbidden words" and seek in their "rebirth" a native land of the future: "Through the words that exist in-between languages we might yet be able to meet" (Andere (W)orte, 2007).

Tzveta Sofronieva's essays and prose, as well as her poetry, are 'earthly', sensuous, sensory and colorful. Michael Speier writes: "Her investigation of the horizons of existence, of the pattern in the carpet of life is one of her particular literary preoccupations. She returns a certain earnestness to contemporary German literature which had gone astray through too much 'coolness'. The gaze comes from the East, … develops out of a coherent whole, a warm and warming biotope."[14]

In *Trost* I learned a new German word from Sofronieva which names the language used in South East European migrants' circles when they want to feel the light, warm wind of their place of origin and speak their own language: a mixture called *Nashenski.*[15]

Where Iliya Troyanov collects and arranges worlds in a purely rational manner, Tzveta Sofronieva seems to gather them on a "family holiday" (as in the end of another short story of hers – *Berlin-Sofia-Berlin,* 2003). She asks questions, questioning herself, too.

The Chamisso prize is a prestigious award given to authors for whom the German language is not native. Adelbert von Chamisso himself is the first "Gastarbeiter" of French origin in the German literature, having enriched its poetry and language with his magnificent work. The contribution of foreign authors introduces new crossing grounds of globalization in literature, a rapprochement of mental worlds, creating the topoi of a mobile society that bears its multiple identities and in which the Bulgarian palimpsest traces its territory.

(Translated by Julia Bouchkova-Maleeva)

Notes

[1] Elias Canetti, *The Tongue Set Free,* p.11.

[2] Iliya Troyanov: *Кучешки времена* (*Hundezeiten*). Balkani Publ. House, Sofia 2008.

[3] Todor Živkov – communist leader of the People's Republic of Bulgaria from 1954 to 1989.

[4] Radev, Milen. *Рентгенов преглед на едно прогнило общество,* in http://www.de-zorata.de/blog/p=97.

[5] The film "A Ballad for Bulgarian Heroes" was produced by Troyanov, Werner von Bergen and Brigitte Ducek and shown on the German channels 3sat and ZDF. In it the author shows political prisoners who have passed through Communist prisons and labour camps.

[6] Elias Canetti: "The Writer's Profession". A speech given in Munich in 1976.

[7] *Die Inschrift* (short stories), 2001; *Engelszungen* (a novel), 2003; *Ein Licht über dem Kopf* (short stories), 2005.

[8] Aleksandar Stambolijski – Prime Minister from 1919 to 1923.

[9] Vanga – legendary Bulgarian fortune-teller.

[10] The *Kakanien* antology can be found at http://www.kakanien.ac/beitr/verb_worte.

[11] The *Verbotene (W)orte* issue of *Transcript* can be found at http://www.transcript-review.org/en/issue/transcript-26-27-forbidden---forbidding-words.

[12] Page references for 'Trost' refer to the German text published in the print anthology *Verbotene Worte* (2005). The English translations are from an unpublished translation by Margot Dembo.

[13] Tzveta Sofronieva has devoted a poem to a similar little snail – "Aplysia" – a genus of sea hares, herbivorous shell-less sea snails, which is used to investigate consciousness ("Bewusst" in *Eine Hand voll Wasser,* 2008: 40).

[14] in: *Wordcatcher: The Poet Tzveta Sofronieva* by Michael Speier, Robert Bosch Foundation Magazine, March/May 2009 (Wortfängerin: Die Dichterin Tzveta Sofronieva. In: Viele Kulturen - eine Sprache, Magazin der Robert Bosch Stiftung, März 2009, pp.10-13)

[15] "And on top of all that a neighbor came by who spoke *Nashenski*. So Anaani found herself in the midst of quite a crowd, which wasn't anybody's fault. Some of them even knew this language that was spoken in Western Europe by southeastern Slavic artists and writers after the dismemberment of Yugoslavia – each speaking his own version of Bulgarian, Croatian, Slovenian, Serbian or Macedonian, respectively, having intense conversations about the war, art, and the world. Although the neighbor had nothing to do with artists and writers, he had grown up in the home of his Yugoslav grandparents who had emigrated to Mecklenburg-Western Pomerania, and he had learned the language there. He had then worked in Thuringia, and after the Berlin Wall came down he started a farm. He rarely spoke *Nashenski* there and was enjoying the opportunity to do so now. Anaani thought, *There is no escape, there is no solution*. But the neighbor did not stay too long." (Consolation, translated by Margot Dembo, p.82)

Bibliography

Canetti, Elias. 1982. 'Der Beruf des Dichters' (The Writer's Profession) in *Das Gewissen der Worte*. Frankfurt/Main: Fischer Taschenbuch Verlag.

— 1977/1994. *Die gerettete Zunge* (*The Tongue Set Free*). Munich: Carl Hanser Verlag.

Dinev, Dimitré. 2003. *Engelszungen*. Wien: Deuticke.

— 2005. *Ein Licht über dem Kopf*. Munich: Hanser.

— 2001. *Die Inschrift*. Wien: Deuticke.

Radev, Milen. Рентгенов преглед на едно прогнило общество. Нов филм на Илия Троянов показва България, каквато германският зрител не е и сънувал. Online at: http://www.de-zorata.de/blog/?p=97.

Sofronieva, Tzveta. 2003. 'Berlin-Sofia-Berlin' in Nicol Ljubic et al. *Feuer, Lebenslust! Erzählungen deutscher Einwanderer*. Stuttgart: Klett-Cotta.

— 2008. *Eine Hand voll Wasser: Deutsche Gedichte*. Aschersleben: Verl. Un Art Ig.

— 1999. *Gefangen im Licht*. Marburg an der Lahn: Biblion.

— 2005. 'Trost' in Verbotene Worte. Munich: Biblion.

Sofronieva, Tzveta. (ed.) 2005. *Verbotene Worte, eine Anthologie über das Gedächtnis der Sprache und die Begegnungen in der Mehrsprachigkeit*. Munich: Biblion.

Sofronieva, Tzveta. Verbotene Worte. Online at: http://www.kakanien.ac.at/beitr/verb_worte.

Speier, Michael. 2009. 'The Poet Tzveta Sofronieva' in Robert Bosch Foundation Magazine, March/May 2009 ('Wortfängerin: Die Dichterin Tzveta Sofronieva' in Viele Kulturen - eine Sprache. Stuttgart: Robert Bosch Stiftung. (pp.10-13).

Troyanov, Iliya/Zeh, Juli. 2009. *Angriff auf die Freiheit. Sicherheitswahn, Überwachungsstaat und der Abbau bürgerlicher Rechte*. Munich: Hanser.

— 2006. Der Weltensammler. (The Collector of Worlds), Munich: Hanser.

— 2006. *Die fingierte Revolution. Bulgarien, eine exemplarische Geschichte*. Munich: Hanser.

— 1996. *Die Welt ist groß und Rettung lauert überall*. Munich: Hanser.

Troyanov, Iliya and Ranjit Hoskote. 2007. *Kampfabsage. Kulturen bekämpfen sich nicht - sie fließen zusammen*. Munich.

Troyanov, Iliya. 2008. Vorwärts und nie vergessen. Online at: http://www.zdf.de/ZDFmediathek/beitrag/video/381598/Vorwaerts-und-nie vergessen%2521#/beitrag/video/381598/Vorwaerts-und-nie-vergessen!

— 2008. *Der entfesselte Globus.* Munich: Hanser.

— 2008. *Kučeški vremena* (tr. Penka Angelova). Sofia: Balkani.

— 2007. *Svetăt e goljam i otvsjakăde debne spasenie* (tr. Gergana Fărkova). Sofia: Siela.

The Water under the Bridge: Tzveta Sofronieva's *Der alte Mann, das Meer, die Frau*

Chantal Wright

Abstract: Tzveta Sofronieva is a poet who writes both in her native language of Bulgarian and in her adopted language of German. Her poetry rejects the notion that it should function as a 'bridge' between cultures, an expectation that arises because of her status as a Chamisso-prize-winning exophonic writer. This essay argues that Sofronieva's recent German poetry is preoccupied with the water under the bridge rather than with the bridge itself: with water as a feminist, non-territorial space; with water as language, water as literature. The chapter focuses its discussion on the poem *Der alte Mann, das Meer, die Frau* (*The old man, the sea, the woman*, 2007), Sofronieva's feminist retelling of Ernest Hemingway's novella *The Old Man and the Sea* (1952).
Keywords: Tzveta Sofronieva, *Adelbert-von-Chamisso-Preis*, exophony, Ernest Hemingway, *The Old Man and the Sea*.

1. Tzveta Sofronieva and the 2009 *Adelbert-von-Chamisso-Preis*

In November 2008, the *Robert Bosch Stiftung* – a German charitable foundation that funds social, educational and intercultural initiatives at home and abroad – announced the winners of the 2009 *Adelbert-von-Chamisso-Preis*. The Chamisso prize has been awarded annually since 1985 and is given to "deutsch schreibende Autoren [...] deren Muttersprache oder kulturelle Herkunft nicht die deutsche ist" (authors writing in German whose mother tongue or cultural background is not German) (Robert-Bosch-Stiftung 2005: 5). Tzveta Sofronieva (1963), a native speaker of Bulgarian, was one of two people recognised with a *Förderpreis*, a prize given to emerging writers who have one full-length publication in German. Sofronieva, who left Bulgaria as a young woman in the tense period that preceded the fall of the Iron Curtain, settled in Germany after a period of global travel and learned the German language as an adult. She was awarded the *Chamisso-Förderpreis* on the basis of her 2008 collection of German-language poetry *Eine Hand voll Wasser* (*A hand full of water*) and for poems and prose texts published in various prominent literary journals including *Akzente* and *Manuskripte*. Sofronieva is already well established as a poet in Bulgaria where she has published since the 1980s.

The six member Chamisso jury praised Sofronieva's poetry in the following terms:

> Ihre genau durchdachten Gedichte, die Stoffe und Motive aus der Antike aufnehmen, stehen in der Tradition einer südosteuropäischen und speziell bulgarischen Lyrik, die die Autorin auf eigenständige, oft anrührende Weise in die deutsche Literatursprache transferiert. (Robert Bosch Stiftung 2008)
>
> (Her precisely thought through poems, which take up themes and motifs from classical antiquity, are in the poetic tradition of South East Europe and particularly Bulgaria, a tradition which the poet transfers into German literary language in her own, often moving way.)[1]

The humanist nature of the Chamisso prize more or less dictates that winners be praised for bridging two cultures and literary traditions. The statement released by the 2009 jury expressed its members' admiration for the novel written by the Argentinian Maria Cecilia Barbetta, who won the other of the two *Förderpreise,* in similar terms: *Änderungsschneiderei Los Milagros* (2008) "gibt der großen lateinamerikanischen Erzähltradition eine neue Heimat in der deutschen Literatur" (ibid.) ('gives the great Latin American narrative tradition a new home in German literature').

The perception of non-native-speaker writers as standard bearers of their native literatures and cultures has been something of a topos since the inception of the Chamisso prize and promotes a narrow critical reception of these authors. Attributing the themes from classical antiquity in Sofronieva's work to the Bulgarian and, more broadly, Balkan tradition, runs the risk of deflecting attention away from other potential origins and functions of these themes. These include the poet's negotiation of her position in a world poetic tradition dominated by men – this is seen most obviously in the poem *Gespräch* (*Conversation*, 2008), in which Sofronieva plays Penelope to Joseph Brodsky's Odysseus – but also the metaphorical access to the elements, and particularly to water, afforded by the gods and heroes of classical mythology. Although Achilles, Orpheus, Odysseus, Zeus, Poseidon and Penelope are all invoked in Sofronieva's poems, countless European and Western poets have invoked them through the ages. When Sofronieva employs the gods in her reflection upon European identity in the era of the European Union (cf. *Als Zeus ihr den Rücken kehrte, 2008) (When Zeus turned his back on her*), it is because Greek mythology is Europe's common literary heritage rather than because Sofronieva was born in the Balkans. The misplaced critical emphasis on the classical motifs in Sofronieva's poetry means that themes of equal if not greater importance in Sofronieva's work are ignored: her dialogue with American and German writers and her fascination with the English language and with American culture; her consideration of male and female societal roles; and perhaps most threateningly for a German readership, her rejection of any territorial claim to language.

The most problematic element of the Chamisso jury's comments, however, is the notion of a "deutsche Literatursprache". This suggests a linguistic mould, into which a Bulgarian or Argentinian or Polish tradition can be poured, and which will put a presentable German face on an alien literature. Forgetting for a moment the erroneous assumption that an exophonic author – an author who writes in an adopted language, usually acquired as an adult[2] – always embodies the literary tradition of his or her country of origin, the phrase "deutsche Literatursprache" implies the existence of a recognisable and in some senses uniform German literary style. The existence and desirability of such a style can be disputed on a number of counts. The first is that literary style is necessarily individual rather than national. This is not to dispute the existence of national stylistic traditions, but merely to concur with Lecercle that style is the result of "the struggle between the writer's own tongue (*sa langue propre*) and the maternal tongue that he tries to appropriate" (Lecercle 1990: 238). The second point of criticism is that exophonic writers are often faced with the task of shaping the German language to their own expressive needs, just as many post-colonial writers took upon themselves the task of shaping the language of the former colonisers to make it suitable for the expression of a post-colonial identity (cf. Ashcroft et al. 2002 [1989]). Exophonic writers have developed a range of strategies for 'appropriating' German (cf. Wright 2007), many of which overlap with the strategies adopted by post-colonial writers, strategies such as the use of neologisms, glossing and the creation of a 'metonymic gap' which deliberately excludes the German reader from the text at certain points (cf. Ashcroft et al. 2002 [1989]). The third point of criticism is that exophonic authors do not simply transfer or translate from one language and literary tradition into another, despite the tendency among German literary critics and among academics to reduce the creativity of these writers to a process of literal translation. Scholars of the Chamisso and Bachmann-prize-winning Turkish-German writer Emine Sevgi Özdamar's work have argued variously that German, for Özdamar, is merely a "literary medium" (Boa 2006: 533), that Özdamar thinks in Turkish and writes in German (Konuk 1997: 150) and that translating Özdamar's German meant "translating a translation" (von Flotow 2000: 65).[3] This assumption fundamentally undermines the literary achievements of exophonic writers by refusing to acknowledge their unique relationship to the German language and the stylistic innovation that results from it.

The literary reception of exophonic writers in Germany, of which the Chamisso prize forms an integral part,[4] has been conditioned by the country's post-war history, its relationship to its ethnic and national minorities and its citizenship laws. A brief literary history of exophonic writers in post-war Germany therefore forms the necessary background to my discussion of Sofronieva's poetry.

2. A brief history of exophonic writing in post-war Germany

The Chamisso Prize, named after Adelbert von Chamisso, a German writer of French origin (1781–1838), was instituted in 1985. Its first winner was Aras Ören, a Turkish actor and poet who moved to Germany in 1969 and spent several years as a *Gastarbeiter* (*'Guest worker'*) in various factories in Berlin. In the same year, the smaller prize for emerging writers was awarded to Rafik Schami, who also worked as a *Gastarbeiter* for several years in the 1970s, and who went on to win the main Chamisso prize in 1993. Today, Schami is one of Germany's bestselling children's authors. The two men entered Germany under the same circumstances as many thousands of foreign workers in the post-war period. The Federal Republic of Germany had been recruiting 'guest' workers since the late 1950s, when its economy boomed as a consequence of post-war investment and the country began to experience a labour shortage. Treaties were signed with a number of countries, including Turkey, Italy and the former Yugoslavia, to encourage the flow of labour into Germany. The Federal Republic's recruitment and treatment of workers did not resemble the socially aware immigration policies that characterise a modern-day immigrant country like Canada. *Gastarbeiter* were seen as a temporary solution to an economic problem: integration and the bestowal of citizenship did not form part of the contemporary discourse surrounding their presence in Germany. Nonetheless, by the late 1970s, when the German government declared a moratorium on recruitment in response to an economic downturn, many *Gastarbeiter* had lived in the Federal Republic for a considerable number of years, had brought their families out to join them there and considered the country their home. Germany's guest worker population was politically disenfranchised. Guest workers had no automatic right to citizenship, as this was still defined ethnically, on the basis of *ius sanguinis*, rather than in terms of *ius soli*, by residence or birthright.

Organisations of worker-writers had begun to spring up in the 1970s. There were attempts on the part of groups such as *Werkkreis Literatur der Arbeitswelt* (*Organisation for Literature of the Workplace*) to encourage German manual labourers to express themselves in writing, and some foreign workers had become involved in these groups. The Italian community in Germany had its own cultural organisations which were funded by the Italian government. It was in this climate that two organisations founded by and for guest workers emerged during the 1980s: *PoLiKunst* and *Südwind gastarbeiterdeutsch*. The aims of these organisations were political: to unite worker-writers of various nationalities and to make the German public aware of the presence of disenfranchised foreign workers in their midst through the adoption of a common literary language – German; to campaign for better rights for foreign workers, including citizenship; and to publish the work of guest worker-writers and concerned Germans in anthologies such as *In neuem Land* (*In New Country*) (Biondi et al. 1980) and *Zwischen Fabrik und Bahnhof* (*Between Factory and Railway Station*) (Biondi et al. 1981). The body of writing produced under the umbrella of these organisations became known as *Gastarbeiterliteratur* (*guest worker literature*). In the same period, the *Institut für Deutsch als Fremdsprache* (*Institute for*

German as a Foreign Language) at the *Ludwig-Maximilians-Universität* in Munich began to organise writing competitions for non-native-speakers of German. The competition entries were published as a series with *Deutscher Taschenbuch Verlag.* Harald Weinrich, who headed the Munich institute, was instrumental in the establishment of the Chamisso prize. In an essay entitled "Um eine deutsche Literatur von außen bittend" (1983) (A plea for German literature from the outside), Weinrich argued that:

> Deutschland ist ein Land, aus Sprache und Geschichte gemacht, und alle Personen, die von der deutschen Sprache einen solchen Gebrauch machen, daß sie diese Geschichte weiterschreiben, sind unsere natürlichen Landsleute, sie mögen von innen kommen oder von außen. (Weinrich 1983, as cited in Robert Bosch Stiftung 2005: 5)

> (Germany is a country formed from language and history, and all those who use the German language in a manner that perpetuates this history are our natural compatriots, whether they come from the inside or beyond.)

In 2009, the Chamisso prize was awarded for the twenty-fifth time. Germany is now a very different country and the writers who receive the Chamisso prize today are a different generation from those early guest-worker writers. A series of legal reforms that began in the 1990s have meant that foreign residents are currently eligible for citizenship after eight years of residence, and that children born in Germany to non-German parents hold dual citizenship until the age of twenty-three, when they are required to choose between their German citizenship and the citizenship of their parent(s). The gradual changes in the law and the fact that writing by non-native speakers had diversified to the point where it could no longer be contained under the umbrellas of *PoLiKunst* and *Südwind*, led to the dissolution of these organisations in the second half of the 1980s. Today, many exophonic writers and German native-speaker writers *mit Migrationshintergrund* (*with a migrational background*) are published by large publishing houses and are the recipients of major German literary prizes. The literary effects of this period in post-war German history are still being felt, however. The humanist overtones of the Chamisso prize have much to do with the early equation of exophonic writing with programmatic *Gastarbeiterliteratur* and the literary struggle for social and legal change. The continued reluctance of many literary critics to acknowledge exophonic writers' stylistic skill and innovation is part of a tradition of reading work by exophonic authors sociologically. The Italian-German poet and novelist Franco Biondi, who was a founding member of *PoLiKunst* and *Südwind*, has argued that *Gastarbeiterliteratur* was accorded a purely sociological reception by critics in order to avoid engaging with it on any other level: "sie abzuurteilen, sie einzuengen in ein bestimmtes Klischee" (to judge it away, to force it into a particular cliché) (von Saalfeld 1998: 147). The tendency to praise Chamisso prize-winners for their bridging of two cultures is part of this same cliché.

3. Reading *Der alte Mann, das Meer, die Frau*

Like the reader of a work translated from a foreign language, the German reader who is not familiar with the Bulgarian and Balkan literary traditions and who has no access to the Bulgarian language is only able to guess at those elements in Sofronieva's work which may have a foreign provenance. He or she lacks the linguistic ability and cultural knowledge to trace their precise origins, and indeed to state with any certainty whether they are dealing with foreign elements that have been translated or transferred from Bulgarian, or whether these elements are grounded in creative use of German or in an investigation of themes which are not simply re-workings of national traditions. In a very few cases, the most obvious being the use of untranslated words and phrases from Sofronieva's mother tongue, the presence of the Bulgarian language is obvious. In the poem *Ein unbekanntes Wort* (*An unknown word*, 2008), the poem becomes iconic of its title, with whole lines printed in un-Romanised Bulgarian, thereby excluding the monolingual reader. This strategy is well documented in post-colonial literary theory as the 'metonymic gap' (cf. Ashcroft et al. 2002 [1989]) – metonymic of the distance between the poet's origins and her readers' current location. In a poem this has a particularly troubling and disabling effect: the Cyrillic script prevents the poem from being read aloud, one cannot even guess at or approximate the pronunciation of the unknown words, and the narrative flow of the poem is interrupted; the Bulgarian words literally create a gap and the reader is prevented from taking possession of the poem. This gap mimics the gap experienced by the speaker of the poem as she contemplates the absence of an equivalent of the German

word *Heimweh* (*homesickness*) in Bulgarian. It also emphasises the
fact that belonging, the notion of home, is not located in language but
in people:

> Der Ort des Bewohnens kann Berlin sein,
> Beverly Hills, Bitterfeld, Konska, Paris.
> Hauptsache es riecht nach Mama (Sofronieva 2008: 20)

> (You can live in Berlin
> Beverly Hills, Bitterfeld, Konska, Paris
> The important thing is that it smells like Mum).

Although, in the example of un-Romanised Bulgarian discussed
above, the foreign element is easily identifiable as such, its meaning
still eludes most readers and it can only be measured in terms of its
poetic effect. This, I would argue, is precisely how Sofronieva's
poetry should be read: in terms of its effect(s) on the monolingual
reader. The precise provenance of these effects may well be
untraceable. Adopting this stance requires that one read the poems as
German texts, and not as translations or as the transferral of one
literary tradition into another language. The cover of *Eine Hand voll
Wasser* does, after all, bear the phrase *Deutsche Gedichte* (*German
Poems*).

Water as a symbol and as a metaphor has been one of the
recurring motifs of Sofronieva's German poetry to date *Konzert*
(*Concert*), *Die Berge, ein Mann, eine Frau* (*The mountains, a man, a
woman*) (2007); *Eine Hand voll Wasser* (*A hand full of water*), *Taufe*
(*Baptism*), *Die Rückkehr des weißen Stiers* (*The return of the white
bull*), *Bewusst* (*Conscious/Aware*) (2008). Water, for Sofronieva,
stands for language and natural languages, it is that which lies under
the bridge that connects two shores, between and around countries, the
element that belongs to nobody but which Western society tries to
bottle, a feminine/feminist space but also a masculine/macho one, a
promise of depth and freedom. Water is the world in which both men
and women exist, separately and together.

In the poem *Der alte Mann, das Meer, die Frau* (*The old man, the
sea, the woman*, 2008), Sofronieva rewrites Hemingway's 1952
novella *The Old Man and the Sea* for the twenty-first century, infusing
Hemingway's symbolism and allegory with feminist energy. In
Sofronieva's retelling, the boy Manolo is present only in the old

man's memory of his youth rather than as a personification of that youth. In the boy's place the woman appears, busy doing housework while the old man goes fishing, contorting herself in high-heeled shoes, reinventing herself, losing and gaining weight, growing older and younger, changing the colour of her hair. She is one woman and she is many; her efforts in the home and with her appearance go unappreciated.

> Sie wechselt ihre Haare, Nationalitäten und Jahre,
> die Breite der Schenkel und der Betten.
> Er bemerkt die Farbe der Bettwäsche nicht.
> [...]
> Sie richtet das Bett mit Wäsche in pompejanischem Rot.
> In seinem Bett rauscht das Meer. (Sofronieva 2007: 263)

> (She changes her hair, nationality and age,
> the width of her thighs and of the bed.
> He doesn't notice the colour of the sheets.
> [...]
> She makes the bed with sheets of Pompeian red.
> In his bed there roars the sea.)

The bombastic red of the bed sheets goes unnoticed, the old man too preoccupied with the sea in his head. Hemingway's allegorical sea is a distant point of reference in this poem: Santiago's epic battle with the noble fish off the shores of Cuba has been reduced in the twenty-first century to a vestigial dream, a hobby. The boat, which sails only in the old man's head, gets a ritual cleaning like a car on Sunday.

> Und der alte Mann ohne das Meer
> rudert sein Boot jede Nacht hinaus in die Weite,
> dürstet nach dem Fisch.
> Und jeden Morgen
> schrubbt er das Boot aufs Neue. (Sofronieva 2007: 263)

> (And the old man without the sea
> rows his boat out every night into the deep,
> thirsts for the fish.
> And each morning
> he scrubs the boat once more.)

The test of masculinity symbolised by Hemingway's sea no longer exists in the new millennium, but as the old man casts around for a new way to communicate with the sea, certain vestigial, gendered behavioural traits remain. The metamorphoses undergone by the woman in the poem are an expression of the pressures women face in Western patriarchal society, pressures which find their locus in women's bodies. These metamorphoses also indicate, however, that women are interchangeable for the old man, and that a woman is an ideal creature rather than a real one. The old man's desire to replace flowers with their scent is a reference to that legendary collector of women, Don Juan, for whom a woman and her scent were one and the same thing.[5] Scent also has Proustian properties. Emasculated twenty-first century man can dream himself elsewhere, into the masculine territory of old, via his sense of smell.

> Manchmal möchte er die Blumen durch ihren Duft ersetzen
> und diesen durch den Jod-Geruch der Algen,
> sie aber durch den Geruch von Fisch, Blut und Meer,
> durch diesen Gestank, in dem die Frau keinen Platz hat. (Sofronieva 2007: 263)

> (Sometimes he'd like to exchange the flowers for their scent
> and this scent for the iodine smell of algae,
> and these for the smell of fish, blood and sea,
> for the stink where the woman has no place.)

If the sea has become no more than a symbol of an extinguished masculinity for the old man, it is something very different for the woman. Santiago reflects on the concept of a masculine and a feminine sea in *The Old Man and the Sea*:

> He always thought of the sea as *la mar* which is what people call her in Spanish when they love her. Sometimes those who love her say bad things of her but they are always said as though she were a woman. Some of the younger fishermen [...] spoke of her as *el mar* which is masculine. They spoke of her as a contestant or a place or even as an enemy. But the old man always thought of her as feminine and as something that gave or withheld great favours, and if she did wild or wicked things it was because she could not help them. The moon affects her as it does a woman, he thought. (Hemingway 1953: 26)

In Hemingway's novella, no matter whether the sea is *la mar* or *el mar*, the gaze upon it is a male one and the possibilities it offers are those of masculine fulfilment. As Grebstein states: "it [the sea] is that sphere in which man becomes most intensely alive, most severely tested, most heroic" (Grebstein 1999: 98). The speaker of Sofronieva's poem asks the question:

Haben die Frau und das Meer eine Geschichte? (Sofronieva 2007: 264)
(Do the woman and the sea have a story?).

The poem is concerned with the female gaze upon the sea, without wishing to negate or ignore the male gaze; it is interested in the other story, the one not told by Hemingway, which the speaker of the poem claims as an equally valid narrative. The poem is also interested in the potential for multiple personal narratives.

Und diese Geschichte ist weder die andere Geschichte
noch ist sie
weniger geschehen
oder jemandem weniger
zugehörig. (Sofronieva 2007: 264)

(And this story is neither the other story
nor did it
happen any less
nor belong
to anybody less.)

This speaks to the conflicting narratives at play within one person's life story, all of them claiming degrees of validity. It also points to the existence of millions of other narratives within millions of other life stories. The transitoriness of the boat upon which the woman finds herself, the whims of the weather and the sea to which the boat is subject, all this symbolises the unpredictability of life, the unexpected events which can take a person to one country or another. Tzveta Sofronieva has been reluctant to commit to a biographical narrative, to an interpretation of events in her life which would reduce a complex, private story to a linear tale fit for public consumption. She stresses instead the multiple interpretations afforded the reader by the literary text. *Der alte Mann, das Meer, die Frau* acknowledges that

[a]ndere Worte bewohnen die anderen Meere. (Sofronieva 2007: 264)
(other words inhabit the other seas.)

Other lives are led, other languages are spoken, other newspapers are read in bed, other stories are possible; the boundaries between one life and other, between one language and another, are fluid and haphazard; the circumstances which lead to one language and place or another are random. In the autobiographical poem *Einbürgerung am Valentinstag*

(*Attaining citizenship on Valentine's Day*, 2008), the poet acknowledges her relationship to the German language and to Germany to be one of chance.

> nur das land meines zufälligen umherirrens
> meiner letzten liebe (Sofronieva 2008: 24)

> (just the country of my chance wanderings
> my latest love).

At this juncture, it is worth stressing that German was not a language that Sofronieva sought out. If anything, then the poet's foreign language of choice was English, which she spoke well at the point when she left Bulgaria. She was conversant with twentieth-century American writers such as Bradbury, Salinger, Steinbeck, Updike, and, of course, Hemingway, all of whose works were accessible in the Bulgaria of the 1980s and whose influence on her writing is considerable. It was only when the focus of Sofronieva's life shifted to Germany in the 1990s that she began to learn German. If Sofronieva's encounter with Hemingway takes place in German then, this is but a matter of chance.

What, however, is the nature of the sea revealed by the female gaze beyond its invocation of instability, its suggestion of shifting narratives, biographies, voices? The female sea is clearly a separate sphere from the sea sailed by men. The woman sees no evidence of the old man's presence while swimming far out in the ocean. The poem tells us that the old man is once again too preoccupied with his fishing to pay attention to the woman. For the woman, the sea is a place of calm, of freedom, she is "entspannt" (relaxed) (Sofronieva 2007: 264), and mermaids await her as she swims out into the open. The symbolism of the mermaids contrasts with that of the male animals that populate Hemingway's writing. Weeks writes:

> Hemingway heroes almost always measure themselves against male animals, whether they are kudu, lions, bear, bulls, or fish. The tragedy enacted in the bull ring becomes a farce if you replace the bull with a cow. The hunter, the torero, the fisherman prove that *they* have *cojones* by engaging another creature that has them beyond dispute. (Weeks 1999: 55)

In Hans Christian Andersen's fairytale *The Little Mermaid* (1836), the little mermaid, a princess of the sea, sacrifices her voice to join her beloved prince on land. The prince promptly falls in love with another woman, thereby unwittingly causing the mermaid's death. In other traditions, the mermaid is a mythical creature reputed to lure sailors and fishermen to their deaths through song. The relationship between men and mermaids is thus a fraught one. In the absence of men, however, mermaids are neither endangered nor do they pose a threat. For Sofronieva, female creatures such as these are homeless and yet at home everywhere in the ocean, a female space. The poem *Bewusst* (*Conscious/Aware*, 2008) tells us of the sea hare Aplysia (sea hares are hermaphrodites, although Sofronieva feminises the adaptable Aplysia here):

> Sie hat kein Haus, schwimmt überall im Ozean
> hat zwanzigtausend, die ihr genügen (Sofronieva 2008: 40)

> (She has no home, swims all through the ocean
> has twenty thousand that suffice).

For the woman in *Der alte Mann*, there is danger out at sea, nonetheless: namely, that the sharks might tire of the old man's fish and feed on the woman instead.

> Doch vielleicht ziehen die raubgierigen Meeresbewohner
> sie dem Fisch des alten Mannes vor
> und schließlich siegt er
> und kehrt immerhin
> mit etwas Fischfleisch nach Hause zurück. (Sofronieva 2007: 264-5)

> (But maybe the rapacious inhabitants of the sea
> will favour her over the old man's fish
> and he conquers finally
> and in the end returns home
> with some fish meat.)

There is in this ending none of the drama of Santiago's return to his village, exhausted, at the point of death, collapsing Christ-like with his mast on his back, the skeleton of the great marlin fastened tight to his boat. In Sofronieva's poem, the old man's victories are small: a little fish meat, the ability – sometimes – to provide his wife's daily bread. The poem's train of thought suggests, however, that the old man is only able to rescue his fish meat from the sharks because the woman distracts them. The success of the fishing expedition thus depends on the woman's sacrifice, and the cost to her is unknown. Santiago's epic struggle with the fish has mutated into a metaphor for marriage, for the relationship between a man and a woman. The woman has replaced the fish, and in this role she becomes the symbol of man's domestication, of his new societal role, a role that no longer demands great feats of bravery, but a solid work ethic instead. The old man struggles with the woman, but her presence defines him and creates a space for him to sail his own sea.

> Manchmal träumt er von ihr, und morgens
> ist er sicher – er hat vom Meer geträumt. (Sofronieva 2007: 265)

> (Sometimes he dreams of her, and in the morning
> is certain – he dreamed of the sea.)

The old man longs for Hemingway's sea, an escape from his everyday life, not realising that his symbolic sea is now located elsewhere. When he returns from the dream sea, awakens from his reverie, there are vestiges of his nocturnal adventure, the same vestiges we see in *The Old Man and the Sea*.

> Das Fischskelett und das Boot.
> Ihre Leere.
> Die Zeitungen. Die Wunden.
> Der Junge und seine Erwartung.
> Die Frau, war sie auch da oder nicht? (Sofronieva 2007: 265)

> (The fish skeleton and the boat.
> Their emptiness.
> The newspapers. The wounds.
> The boy and his expectation.
> The woman, was she there too or not?)

The skeleton of the marlin, the emptiness of the boat, the newspapers that line Santiago's bed, the wounds inflicted by the fishing line and the long days under the sun, the boy's expectations: all these are present in Sofronieva's "Old Man" too, it is only the woman's participation in the fishing expedition that is in doubt. What is the role of the unmentioned female 'other' in Hemingway's tale of masculinity, the poem appears to be asking. Hemingway defines masculinity on its own terms, without reference to its binary opposite. The only woman in *The Old Man and the Sea* is *la mar*, but the sea's behaviour in the eye of the beholder can change its gender: it is masculine when behaving as a competitor or a foe, feminine when it bestows favours or visits evil upon those who sail it. Perhaps both Hemingway's and Sofronieva's old men are concerned that their gender might change when their behaviour is beheld by society; Hemingway's old man seems to have internalised the societal gaze, he behaves 'like a man' even without an audience; Sofronieva's poem suggests that the societal gaze is a combination of genetics and evolution, more a matter of nature than cultural conditioning, that gender is pre-programmed. Either way, both writers sympathise with the old man's struggle.

> Allmählich beginnt der alte Mann zu glauben,
> dass der Kampf mit dem Fisch, der Junge
> und sogar die Frau
> keine Aufgabe sind,
> sondern ein Code im Körper. (Sofronieva 2007: 265)

> (Gradually the old man starts to believe
> that the struggle with the fish, the boy
> and even the woman
> are not a task
> but a code in the body.)

The role played by genetics in the constitution of the human being is a matter of professional interest to Sofronieva – she is a physicist by training and holds a doctorate in the history of science – but it is also a topos in contemporary German poetry. Durs Grünbein's poem *Grauzone Morgens* (1988), from the collection of the same name, also questions the extent to which human beings' acceptance of the routine of their daily lives is a matter of genetic pre-programming. Grünbein's portrait of the grey, monotonous, and in all likelihood East German city, through which commuters move unquestioningly, uses a train motif to symbolise the unthinking observance of mind-numbing routine and the impossibility of escape.

> all der funkelnden Schienen an die
>   geheftet du durch den Tag
>   gleitest, als wäre
>
> Zeit nicht diese genetische Droge oder
>   irgendein Code für den

> unmerklichen Junkie-Rhythmus im Blut. (Grünbein 1988: 14)

(all the glistening tracks
    stapled to which you glide
        through the day as if

time were not this genetic drug or
    some kind of code for the
        impalpable junkie rhythm in the blood)

Both Sofronieva and Grünbein use the word "Code", both of them discuss key organising principles of society – time, marriage – in terms of an involuntary, genetic reflex. Grünbein's view, however, is apocalyptic where Sofronieva's is melancholy. In the same poem, he goes on to write of the horror people would experience if their brains could somehow be exposed to the true nature of the world around them:

Stell dir vor: ein Café voller Leute, alle
    mit abgehobenen Schädeldecken, Gehirn
        bloßgelegt
            (Dieses Grau!) und dazwischen
nichts mehr was eine Resonanz auf den
        Terror ringsum
            dämpfen könnte

[Picture this: a café full of people, all of them
    with their skulls flipped open, brain
        exposed
            (The grey!) and in-between
nothing that could muffle
    a response
        to the terror all around].

4. Conclusion: The water under the bridge

In *Der alte Mann, das Meer, die Frau*, the water of the sea is a feminist space, a place where woman swims free and unobserved by man. But water is also language unfettered by territorial associations. It is no particular national language: not Bulgarian, not German, not English, simply language. In the poem *Donnerstag: Viadukt* (*Thursday: Viaduct*) (forthcoming), the speaker of the poem describes the bridge function imposed upon her and the contortions this necessitates. This time it is not the contortions visited upon woman by female societal roles, but the contortion that comes from the immense effort of linking one shore with another.

> Über mich gehen viele Räder und Menschen
> meine Arme und Beine sind gestreckt
> mit Nägeln, festgekrallt in den Sanddünen
> meine Wirbel knacken nicht
> wer hinübergeht kann ich nicht sehen
> mein Gesicht starrt ins Wasser: Siddhartas Fluss. (Sofronieva, forthcoming)

> (Many wheels and people cross over me
> my arms and legs are stretched
> with nails, dug into the sand dunes
> my vertebrae do not crack
> I cannot see who is passing by
> my face stares into the water: Siddharta's river.)

Other people demand of the poet that she transfer, translate, bridge. The poet herself is studying the river, like Siddhartha in his quest for enlightenment. The people crossing the poet's human bridge miss out on the water underneath. For Siddhartha, to study the water under the bridge was to study life, for the poet, literature, freed from national constraints. This is the poet's plea for readers to pay attention to her work rather than to her nationality or her biography, her plea to be freed from what Cheesman has referred to as "the burden of representation" (Cheesman 2006).[6] This does not indicate that Sofronieva is indifferent to the language(s) in which she writes, nor is this part of a wider humanist claim that all languages and peoples are the same. At the very minimum, each language has a distinct physiology that is worthy of investigation. In the poem *Über das Glück nach der Lektüre von Schopenhauer, in Kalifornien* (*On happiness after reading Schopenhauer, in California*, 2007), Sofronieva plays with the different sounds in the Bulgarian, German and English words for 'happiness/luck'.

> Es gibt viele Lücken im Glück,
> auch verrückt und bedrückt stecken im luck.
> Im Bulgarischen wird das Glück, schtastie, oft verschluckt,
> viel *sch* und *t*, viel *scht*,
> Schweigen ist im Glück,
> auch viel *st*, Angst, Steine, Stolpern, Stolz, Stelle, Stop.

Das Phänomen schtastie und sein Verschlucken im Hals
sind so angenehm zu erforschen. (Sofronieva 2007: 259)

(Happiness has its lacunae,
the English word *luck* with its *u* like an *a*,
lacquer that conceals, a layering.
In Bulgarian happiness is *shtastie*, you choke on it,
all that *sh*, all that *shh*,
silence, there is silence in happiness.
And also plenty of *st*, a fear that sets in, stagnant, static, stigmata, steppe, stop.
The phenomenon of *shtastie*, the way it sticks in the throat
is pleasant to consider.) (trans. Quintavalle 2007)

The German exophonic writer Yoko Tawada, whose mother tongue is
Japanese and who, like Tzveta Sofronieva, writes in both her native
and adopted languages, displays a similar fascination with those
aspects of language that go beyond the communicative. Tawada's
exploration of the materiality of language in such essays as "Von der
Muttersprache zur Sprachmutter" (From the Mother Tongue to the
Tongue Mother, 1996) and "Sieben Geschichten der sieben Mütter"
(Seven Stories of the Seven Mothers, 1996) is facilitated by her
encounter with the foreign and the awareness of difference which
results from this encounter. In other words, her preoccupation with the
surface structure of language develops out of the realisation that there
are co-existent Saussurean systems. A comparison of surface signs
leads back to a comparison of their associated signifieds. This is
precisely what Sofronieva is doing in *Über das Glück*: the German
word 'Glück' can signify both 'happiness' and 'luck'. Which of the
two meanings is implied has to be induced from the context; the Los
Angelean Venice is a linguistic translation of the Italian city Venezia,
but as Venice changes language, it undergoes significant physical and
cultural transformation too. Different languages have different
possibilities. Thus, although it is the water under the bridge that
counts, the shores on either side of the water are not without
significance:

Die Behältnisse zur Aufbewahrung des Glücks
sind offenbar von Bedeutung. (Sofronieva 2007: 259)

(For happiness to keep
you need the right container.) (tr. Quintavalle 2007)

Der alte Mann, das Meer, die Frau illustrates the paucity of a reading strategy that would handle exophonic texts as though they were bridges from one literary tradition to another. Sofronieva's poem channels Hemingway, the American modernist, not Balkan folk traditions. It considers how male and female relationships function, caught between the nominal equality of the twenty-first century and genetic gender overhang. It investigates the metaphorical possibilities of water: a non-territorial, extra- and intra-linguistic space. To reduce Sofronieva's poetry to a bridging function is to do a great disservice to its poetic richness and to rob it of its signifying possibilities.

Notes

[1] Throughout this chapter, unless otherwise indicated, all translations from the German are my own.

[2] On the emergence and application of the term 'exophonic', see Arndt and Naguschewski and Stockhammer (2007); Wright (2008).

[3] Dayıoğlu-Yücel (2005: 133) also cites the influential literary critic Marcel Reich-Ranicki's discussion of Özdamar's novel *Die Brücke vom Goldenen Horn* ('*The Bridge of the Golden Horn*') (1998) in the television show *Das Literarische Quartett* (shown on ZDF on 6 June 1998), in which Reich-Ranicki dismissed Özdamar's creativity as almost entirely the result of literal translation.

[4] The Chamisso prize is open to writers from any of the German-speaking countries. Nonetheless, it is administered in Germany and overwhelmingly awarded to writers who are based in that country.

[5] In Mozart's opera *Don Giovanni*, which is based on the Don Juan legend, Don Giovanni identifies the approach of Donna Elvira by her smell: "Zitto! Mi pare sentir odor di femmina!" ('Hush! I seem to smell femininity!') (Bleiler 1964: 95). The reference to the Don Juan legend was pointed out to me by the poet in personal correspondence.

[6] Cheesman uses this expression in the context of a discussion of German-Turkish novelists and the ways in which they react to pressures to represent or engage with the German-Turkish experience.

Bibliography

Andersen, Hans Christian. 2004. *Fairy Tales* (tr. Tiina Nunnally). New York: Penguin.

Arndt, Susan, Dirk Naguschewski and Robert Stockhammer. 2007. *Exophonie.* Berlin: Kulturverlag Kadmos.

Ashcroft, Bill, Gareth Griffiths and Helen Tiffin. 1989/2002. *The Empire Writes Back*, 2nd edn. London: Routledge.

Barbetta, Maria Cecilia. 2008. *Änderungsschneiderei Los Milagros.* Frankfurt am Main: Fischer.

Boa, Elizabeth. 2006. 'Özdamar's Autobiographical Fictions: Trans-National Identity and Literary Form' in *German Life and Letters* 59(4): 526–539.

Biondi, Franco et al. (eds). 1980. *In neuem Land.* Bremen: CON.

— (eds). 1981. *Zwischen Fabrik und Bahnhof.* Bremen: CON.

Cheesman, Tom. 2006. 'Juggling Burdens of Representation: Black, Red, Gold and Turquoise' in *German Life and Letters* 59(4): 471–487.

Dayıoğlu-Yücel, Yasemin. 2005. *Von der Gastarbeit zur Identitätsarbeit. Integritätsverhandlungen in türkischen-deutschen Texten von Şenocak, Özdamar, Ağaoğlu und der Online-Community* vaybee! Göttingen: Universitätsverlag Göttingen.

Grebstein, Sheldon Norman. 1970. 'Hemingway's Craft in *The Old Man and the Sea*' in Bloom, Harold (ed.) *The Old Man and the Sea.* Philadelphia: Chelsea House: 95-103.

Grünbein, Durs. 1998. *Grauzone Morgens.* Frankfurt am Main: Suhrkamp.

Hemingway, Ernest. 1952. *The Old Man and the Sea.* London: The Reprint Society.

Konuk, Kader. 1997. 'Das Leben ist eine Karawanserei: Heim-at bei Emine Sevgi Özdamar' in Ecker, Gisela (ed.) *Kein Land in Sicht: Heimat-weiblich?* München: Fink: 143–157.

Lecercle, Jean-Jacques. 1990. *The Violence of Language.* London: Routledge.

Mozart, Wolfgang Amadeus. 1964. *Don Giovanni* (tr. Ellen H. Bleiler). New York: Dover.

Özdamar, Emine Sevgi. 1998. *Die Brücke vom Goldenen Horn.* Köln: Kiepenheuer & Witsch.

Robert Bosch Stiftung. 2005. *Viele Kulturen – Eine Sprache. Adelbert-von-Chamisso Preisträgerinnen und Preisträger 1985 – 2005.* Stuttgart: Robert Bosch Stiftung.

— 2008. 'Adelbert-von-Chamisso-Preis 2009 für Artur Becker'. Online at: http://www.bosch-stiftung.de/content/language1/html/21241.asp   (consulted 14/10/2009).

Sofronieva, Tzveta. 2007. 'Gedichte' in *Akzente* Heft 3, Juni 2007.

— 2008. *Eine Hand voll Wasser.* Aschersleben: Unartig.

— (forthcoming). 'On happiness after reading Schopenhauer, in California', (tr. Rufo Quintavalle).

— (forthcoming). 'Donnerstag: Viadukt'.

Tawada, Yoko. 1996. *Talisman.* Tübingen: Konkursbuchverlag Claudia Gehrke.

Von Flotow, Luise. 2000. 'Life is a Caravanserai: Translating Translated Marginality, a Turkish-German *Zwittertext* in English' in *Meta* 45(1): 65–72.

Von Saalfeld, Lerke. (ed.). 1998. *Ich habe eine fremde Sprache gewählt.* Gerlingen: Bleicher.

Weeks, Robert P. 1962. 'Fakery in *The Old Man and the Sea*' in Bloom, Harold (ed.) *The Old Man and the Sea.* Philadelphia: Chelsea House: 53-9.

Weinrich, Harald. 1983. 'Um eine deutsche Literatur von außen bittend' in *Merkur* 37: 911-920.

Wright, Chantal. 2007. *Translating the exophonic text. The German prose writings of Franco Biondi, Emine Sevgi Özdamar and Yoko Tawada.* PhD thesis. UEA Norwich.

— 2008. 'Writing in the "grey zone". Exophonic literature in contemporary Germany' in *GfL – German as a Foreign Language* 3/2008: 26–42.

Goran Stefanovski – A Playwright in the Tower of Babel

Goce Smilevski

Abstract: In *Reflections on Exile* Edward Said states that the exiles have contrapuntal vision of culture and are aware of its simultaneous dimensions. This text is focused on examining the relation of the characters of Goran Stefanovski's plays towards culture, identity, and the playwright's playful use of the dichotomy of collectivism and individualism as the stereotypes of Eastern and Western Europe.
Keywords: Goran Stefanovski, Edward Said, exile, identity, stereotypes, Eastern and Western Europe.

1. The Lost Stories in Hotel Europa

In *Reflections on Exile* Edward W. Said states: "Most people are principally aware of one culture, one setting, one home; exiles are aware of at least two, and this plurality of vision gives rise to an awareness of simultaneous dimensions, awareness that – to borrow a phrase from music – is contrapuntal. […] There is a unique pleasure in this sort of apprehension" (Said 2001: 186). The play *Hotel Europa* by Goran Stefanovski (born in Bitola, 1952) reveals the bitterness of this *unique pleasure*, and the audience is witnessing it since its beginning, when in a steamy atmosphere of a stuffy room, in the hotel "Europa", a woman that is knitting says (actually – recitates): "We are children of Latvia. We came to the West one summer, many moons ago, to earn some money, to make our ends meet. We worked on the fields, we helped with the harvest. Time passed on. And then we stayed. They put us in this hotel. And then they forgot about us" (p.4).

Hotel Europa is a play about remembrance and forgetting, about the struggle for keeping one's own identity and about its loss. It is a space where appear Odysseus and an Eastern European entrepreneur, Circe and a drifter woman, angels and bodyguards…, telling their stories or trying to escape from them. As these stories are fragments of the past of the characters, *Hotel Europa* sets on stage subjects that are (re)constituted in the process of a clash between their tradition and the new cultural surrounding. Some of them, in their attempt to reconstruct their broken lives, face the arrogant ignorance of the Other: "HUSBAND: These bastards asked me where I was from. Latvia, I said! Where the fuck is that, they said? I'll show you where it is, I said! (HE SHOWS HIS HEART) Here! I said. This is where "the fuck" it is I said! And fuck you too! Next thing I know - I'm fighting these six big motherfuckers" (p.5). This character is not able to give up his national pride, and at the same time he is not able to convince even himself of the reason why is he proud. The name of his native country becomes a metaphor for himself, but he is not aware, or he has forgotten, or he is not able to express in words, what lays beyond that metaphor. Being in exile, he has lost his old story, but he has not found a new one. Edward Said says that "[e]xile is strangely compelling to think about but terrible to experience. It is the unhealable rift forced between a human being and a native place […] and while it is true that literature and history contain heroic, romantic, glorious, even triumphant episodes in an exile's life, they are no more than efforts meant to overcome the crippling sorrow of estrangement" (p.173). Stefanovski's plays never contain heroic, romantic, glorious, nor triumphant episodes in an exile's life. *Hotel Europa, Casabalkan, Tatooed Souls,* are about *the crippling sorrow of estrangement*, mixed with some irony.

2. The Playwright and His Story

In 2004 Goran Stefanovski was discussing a topic for his speech with his friends from the Hamburg International Summer Festival. They suggested the topic *Why the East is not sexy any more?* Their idea provoked him to write the speech *Stories from the Wild East*. It is an essay on stories, memory and loss of identity. Explaining the term *story,* Stefanovski says that it "is a narrative. An account. A sequence of events. It tells us who we are, who we have been, who we could become. It is an interpretation." Stefanovski links it with "identity, which is also a story of who we think we are, a constant negotiation and renegotiation of self. Like theatre, which likewise is a reflection, a vision of the world and oneself, a reading of the past and a projection of the future" (Stefanovski 2005: 70). He also tells his own story:

> My name is Goran Stefanovski. This is the story of my life in a few short sentences. I was born in the Republic of Macedonia, which, at that time, was part of the Federative Republic of Yugoslavia. My father was a theatre director and my mother was an actress. I spent my first 40 years in Skopje as a playwright and a teacher of drama. I married Pat, who's English. We had two children and we were happy. We had a good story. Then, in 1991, the Yugoslav civil wars started. Our lives took a sharp U-turn. Pat decided that the future of the Balkans wasn't going to be the future of our children. They moved to England. I started commuting between Skopje in Macedonia, where my secure past and my greater family were, and Canterbury in England, where my uncertain future and my nuclear family were. I started living between two stories. *We've lost our story*, I told Pat. *No*, she said, *the story has lost us* (p. 64–65).

Stefanovski's statement "I spent my first 40 years in Skopje as a playwright and a teacher of drama" needs a footnote. At the end of the 1970s and in the 1980s, he grew into one of the most prominent playwright figures of Eastern Europe, and his plays were awarded at many relevant national and international theatre festivals. He also wrote the script for the TV serial *The Crazy Alphabet*, a genuine introduction for children into the world of letters, but it wasn't watched by children only: it had a wide audience, age 5 to 95. His play *Wild Flesh* (premiered in Skopje on 29/12/1979), is claimed to be an opening of a new chapter in the theatre history of Yugoslavia, a country whose story was about to end just a little more than a decade later. After moving with his family to Canterbury, the story of his life had a new chapter. In his speech given on the occasion of becoming a member of the Macedonian Academy of Sciences and Arts in 2004, he gave us a glimpse into his exile. It was not heroic, romantic, glorious, nor triumphant. It was told with irony (especially about the gap between the expectations he had as an author, and the reality), and beyond it can be heard *the crippling sorrow of estrangement*: "I am already in depression, I already miss myself. I'd get on an ant's back, to get me back home. [...] Well, where is the invitation from the Queen? Well, I expected tea-time, Lords, Ladies and bon-ton" (2005: 19). One of these sentences ("I'd get on an ant's back, to get me back home") echoes the words told in *Tattoed Souls* (1984). The characters of Stefanovski's plays have faced the exile (or desired it) much before their creator moved from Skopje to Canterbury. In *Wild Flesh,* settled in Skopje before the Second World War, where the tragedy of a family precedes the tragedy of the world, Stevo dreams of Berlin, Hamburg, Marburg and Würzburg. Voidan, the main character of *Tattoed Souls,* is an ethnologist that goes to USA to do research for his Master's thesis *The influence of migration processes on the mental and physical constitution of Macedonian immigrants in the United Stats of America.* Ione in *Long Play* (1988) dreams to leave Macedonia and to become the fifth *Beatles.* In *The Tower of Babel* (1989), Damian refuses the opportunity to immigrate to Canada, Marta desires to leave for London, and Rina returns to Macedonia, after years of exile. Stefanovski characterizes *The Tower of Babel* as "an attempt at an analysis of our unconscious" (2005: 103). It is also a play about memory and forgetting, like most of his works.

3. The Black Hole of Our Time

When I travel abroad, I often meet people who say they don't know where Macedonia is on the map. I guess I am lucky, for I always meet nice people, and they never say, like those in *Hotel Europa*: "Where the fuck is that?" They usually ask me about *the story* of the country I come from. From the way they ask the question, I can tell they need a short and quick answer, so I am trying to satisfy them and I reply with one line: They should read Stefanovski's plays, some twenty pieces. I can see they are disappointed, for they wanted a simple, short sentence, that would be an answer and not a reference, they needed something that they would keep 'forever' in the folder for geography in their brain, linked with the term Macedonia. Of course, I cannot be angry about the fact that they are not *really* interested in *our story*. I suppose that they are equally without interest in *their own story* – and when they know it, it is made usually of a few short, consize sentences.

Trying to understand our approaches to *someone's* story, we can go back to Stefanovski's *Stories from the Wild East.* There he speaks about the grand stories, about the master narratives. They "create the social context and intellectual discourse in which an artist operates. They are the centrifugal forces of society and culture. The artist can take it or leave it, but the context is there. Like gravity" (2005: 72). Stefanovski observes Eastern and Western European basic stories as two opposite master narratives. The Western European is founded on individualism par excellence, it is "the bastion of political sterility and metaphysical failure" and its final result is "greed and consumerism" (p.74-5). The Eastern European story is based on patriarchal collectivism: "Individualisation comes at a deadly price" (p.73). That is why Silyan, in Stefanovski's play *The Black Hole* (1987), desires a different life, in different cultural surrounding: "There'll be no me there any more. No name, no past, no future. No tradition. No morality. I won't owe anybody anything. I won't expect anything. I'll just <u>be</u>" (p.29). At the same time, he is aware of the final result of this desire for escape: "We vanish. Cease to exist. This sofa, this room, this town, this language we speak, the square, the people, their habits and customs, all the files, newspapers, dishes and drinks. All swept away. Vanished. Into thin air" (p.12). The question is – is there (in the Eastern European story) a possibility for a third way – neither cruel collectivism, nor escapism. Or it is too late for that answer, as the choice is being made? Stefanovski discusses this problem in *Stories from the Wild East*:

> When Indiana Jones goes 'out there', he doesn't go to any particular history or geography. He goes to a jumbled-up Third World, full of greasy losers, mostly without a face, and mostly killed wholesale. Because Hollywood doesn't make room for geography and history, Eastern European artists do not feel properly represented. So they yearn to supply their history and geography. Their own map of the world. Their own compass. But here lies the trap which makes them obsolete. Their kids who go to the cinema are between 18 and 22 and they don't care about geography and history. They care about Indiana Jones (p.81-2).

Beginning with his first play *Jane Zadrogaz*, premiered in Skopje on 27/12/1974, a postmodern approach to folklore, with a subtitle: "A Folk Fantasy with Singing", and his latest one produced in Macedonia, "The Demon from Debar Maalo" (premiered in Skopje in 2006), about the city's identity loss (Debar Maalo is a quarter in Skopje), Stefanovski's plays have the cultural memory as one of their subjects, and at the same time, they are cultural memory themselves. In them, Stefanovski diagnoses the black hole of our time – the collective amnesia born out of the loss of one's own story and the disinterestedness for the story of the Other. That is the sickness of our contemporary Tower of Babel, our global world. The answer to the question posed by Boris in *HI-FI* (1982): "Can people be 'hi-fi'? True to themselves?" (p.23), may be that being true to oneself is in the constant questioning of one's own identity, a search into oneself and one's own tradition in relation to the identity of the Other, and the tradition of Others. The time of cultural amnesia is a negation of the self, a hipertrophy of individualisation without real individual. It is a time, when questions like those of Mihailo from *Flying on the Spot* (1981) are impossible: "And what if there are other frescoes under these? And more under them? And yet more under those? Where are the *real* ones? Which are mine? *(He looks at his coat.)* There is something else under this. *(He takes it off).* And under this? *(He takes his shirt off.)* And under this? *(He is left naked to the waist. He grabs hold on his skin.)* And under this? What's under this? Where is Mihailo?" (p.183).

Bibliography

Said, Edward. 2001. *Reflections on Exile and Other Essays*. Cambridge: Harvard University Press.

Stefanovski, Goran. 1985a. 'Flying on the Spot' (tr. Patricia Marsh-Stefanovska) in *Scena*, English issue 8: 170-88.

— 1985b. *HI-FI & The False Bottom.* (tr. Patricia Marsh Stefanovska). University of Missouri, Kansas City: BkMk Press.

— 1987. *The Black Hole* (tr. Patricia Marsh-Stefanovska). Manuscript.

— 2000. *Hotel Europa.* Manuscript.

— 2003. *Prikazni ot Diviot Istok (Tales from the Wild East)*. Skopje: Tabernakul. Online translation available at: http://www.diversity.org.mk/Sodrzini.asp?idEKniga=54.

Fragments Between Desire and Nostalgia: A Macedonian Case

Maja Bojadžievska

Abstract: A cluster of topics which reaches beyond the vision of the seductive encounter between texts/cultures can be viewed through a specific 'Macedonian' case of prose fiction, the novel *Snow in Casablanca* by Kica B. Kolbe – a philosopher and novelist. Kolbe's novel reflects the images of a double refugee. Her prose exploits the notion of translation through Walter Benjamin's concept of translation as a "migrant's dream of survival." Between nostalgia and desire, between the 'old home' which was never one and the new home which is always already provisional, between 'the place' of her native country which never got a real name (Fyrom) and 'the place' of aesthetic idolatry (Europe), Kolbe's novel redresses the questions of cultural alterity, opens up new spaces by performing different and playful artistic rites of secrecy around the old identity cores.
Keywords: cultural translation, expatriate, exile, refugee, nostalgia, placelessness, diaspora, cultural myth, scent, quest, memorialization.

Today, the processes and diverse conditions of human migrancy are such that they widen to a great extent the range of the cultural go-betweens.

It is widely agreed that the translation has become central to cultural history and therefore, literary texts are not seen as constituted primarily of language but, in fact, of culture, language being in effect the vehicle of culture. If it is true that the term *cultural translation* was originally coined by the anthropologists in the circle of Edward Evans Pritchard "to describe what happens in cultural encounters when each side tries to make sense of the actions of the other" (Burke 2005/6), then literary scholars have to admit that the tracking of the ways in which texts traverse the boundaries of national literatures, 'homogenous', and 'authentic' cultures and of literary genre – turns back again in the anthropological zone.

Some of the basic questions opened up by the cultural translation refer to a whole 'aggregate' of phenomena which are present in the works of the South Eastern European (diaspora) writers, especially after 1990.

The shared post-communist universe was certainly not a space of desired, voluntary encounter between two or more traditions in the frame of some peaceful, utopian horizon, but a space where the experience of displacement (and therefore, identities-in-translation) was the result of conflicts, economic devastations and different forms of violence. Thus, the new, mobile identities which emerge from local and global traumas are, ultimately, deeply marked by the dystopian world of an unwanted kind.

A cluster of topics which certainly reaches beyond the vision of the seductive encounter between texts/cultures can be viewed through a specific Macedonian 'case': the novel *Snow in Casablanca* by Kica B. Kolbe, a philosopher, scholar, translator and novelist.

Kica Kolbe's novel reflects the images of a double refugee. A child of ethnic Macedonians driven from their homes in northern Greece during the civil war in Greece (1948/1949), she experienced, from her present point of view,[1] only a temporary, conditional 'placedness' and, consequently, a conditional sense of identity in the years of living in Ex-Yugoslav Macedonia, until her second migration, this time to Germany, in 1985. Primarily a university philosophy teacher, she becomes a writer only after the 1990s. The first book she published in the late 1990s was not fiction, but primarily a kind of family history, a confession which deals with the problems of a historically grounded, real collective trauma of the Macedonians forced to leave their homes in northern Greece (Kolbe, 1999).

Raised in a family of former refugees in a small house near the railway at the outskirts of Skopje, she was caught up in the vision of the home her parents dreamed of which, meanwhile, has become a narrative home, while the former 'real' one was, for political reasons, beyond their reach. However, the problematic concept of home for these refugees was even more threatened by the quiet and 'subtle' exclusion they experienced together in the former Yugoslavia as 'Aegeans' (*Egejci*), which constructed them as 'others' for the 'real' Macedonians. This certainly led to a radical interrogation of identity in Kolbe's first book, conceived and written in her old/new home, and published in her old/new state, the Republic of Macedonia in 1999.

Unable to identify herself with anywhere in particular, unable to find recourse in the framing concept of the Nation-State, Kolbe later becomes one of the rare authors in Macedonia who were ready to challenge the narratives of belonging to a particular form of identity. This becomes visible in her novel *Snow in Casablanca* where Kolbe, generally speaking, redresses the questions of the expatriates, exiled persons, the questions of not-belonging, finding ground in the experience of alienation. Her experience as a philosophy teacher at the University in Skopje, as well as her scholarly work on Kant (examining his reflections on nostalgia) and especially on authors like Theodor Adorno and Walter Benjamin (both Jews by origin) was surely connected to her personal sense of alienation as a definitive *conditio* of modernity.

The main character in Kica Kolbe's novel, Dina, is a young, well educated woman, a child of refugees, ethnic Macedonians from northern Greece. Her parents migrated to Canada in the 1990s, this time due to economic reasons, carrying a deep feeling of disappointment and fear. The second 'home' in their third 'fatherland' (because it turns out that they have changed at least three states: Greece, Yugoslavia and, after 1991, the independent Republic of Macedonia) is not left behind, but dragged with them, to Canada, as Joyce would say, "as new second hand clothes", reproducing itself, again in narration.

If we follow the elucidations made by Svetlana Boym, Dina's parents are doubled and tripled dreamers, whose nostalgia is reflexive. As Boym points out, the reflexive nostalgia does not reconstruct the national past, but is connected to individual and cultural memory, invoking the broken fragments of remembrance, restoring space and time, being in love with distance, with the longing, and not with the object of that longing.

Although the affliction of the refugees is an effect of political go-betweens, in their "leisure hours" (Burke), they become cultural go-betweens, or... if we want to be emphatic, cultural translators. Another concept allied to the cultural translation is 'negotiation', a concept which has expanded and moved far beyond the domains of politics and trade. Negotiation refers to the exchange of ideas and the mutual modification of meaning and thus, the reflection on consequences of 'cultural encounters' is, in fact, a reflection on the double process of decontextualization and recontextualization – a process which is crucial for the refugees seen as cultural translators. It has been pointed out by a group of literary scholars that even the act of understanding can be seen as a kind of translation, a kind of modifying and altering other people's concepts and domesticating them in one's own vocabulary. Thus, the refugees in a figurative sense of the word are in the position of negotiators between two or more cultures.

Their repetitive movements along the arrival/settlement/return axis are certainly not arranged in a direction of building a new, even mythic home (literal and metaphorical), but they work as a counter-narrative of the traditional, national narratives which, in principle, reflect the firm concepts of a homogenous territory and stable national identity. From this point of view, Kolbe's prose shows to a certain extent how the conditional and indecisive ethnocentrism of her parents has melted down, faced with the recognition of the overall human condition of the problematicity in the world: "Once a refugee – always a refugee," says Dina's father. The inability of Dina's parents to fabricate and consolidate the identity of their wider group at a national level raises several questions whose answering will later be a part of their daughter's endeavor.

These questions are in a certain way related to the reflections of the Italian philosopher Giorgio Agamben (Agamben 2000). For the Western political imagination, the identity of the refugee is a non-identity, and his/her life is a non-life. As Agamben points out, bearing in mind that the status of the refugee is *outside* the nation state, it should be considered as a limit-concept which, consequently, challenges not only the very principle of the nation-state but, furthermore, reveals the problematic concept of *place*. In the 20th and 21st centuries, the political issue of the displaced persons has been transformed into an ontological issue. The affront the displaced persons pose to the idea of Nation-state – if we follow the philological origin of *nascita*: 'birth', "which implies that for those born within the national boundaries, the Nation itself functions as origin and definition" (Kelly 2007) – is defined with the lack of capacity of the Western *polis* to incorporate the refugees, to integrate them or better, to *place* them. The refugees, says Agamben, as external to the nation-state, become identifiable only with a 'mass-phenomenon', but they should be seriously considered as a "limit concept that at once brings a radical crisis to the principles of the nation state and clears the way for a renewal of categories that can no longer be delayed". What

Agamben implicitly proposes further in his text is a renewal or at least, reconceptualization of *place*.

Developing the reflection on the complexity of the translation's relation to place, Stephen Kelly believes that a specific space is, in fact, organized imaginatively as a *multiplicity of places* and, following the thought of Hana Arendt, he imagines place as constituted by the "infinite plurality and differentiation of human beings". Consequently, the histories and the desires of the human being wrap their roots around the spaces, the 'soils' they occupy; however, only for the refugee, that soil is contested.

On the other hand, if we compare the motivations for Dina's migration with the migration of her parents, there is a great difference. At the beginning of the novel, we see Dina more as a figure of a voluntarily exiled person. Her migration to Europe is not a consequence of a civil war but, in fact, a matter of individual choice. For her, placelessness is not the result of a collective affliction, because she describes her life as a sort of a pilgrimage:

> The child, for whose sake they sacrificed everything in life, left its parents there, in the diaspora and set out to wander around, searching for some holy places which I only imagined reading literature. (p.32)

Dina sees herself as a virtual refugee, because she once set out for the 'northwest' of Europe, following her desire for the worshiped, ideal family of European writers and artists. This spiritual/artistic kinship she seeks makes Europe a referential universe of a specific aesthetic idolatry. Europe as a cultural myth is not a new idea for the eastern and south European writers and intellectuals, who like Kolbe, have chosen dislocation rather than attachment, leaving behind all the certainties solemnized and sanctioned by their respective national histories and heritages. Dina changes her old fatherland, the old "glasshouse," an already virtual world of decomposed ideas and vestiges, throwing away the traditional concepts of fatherhood and legitimacy: "For me, fatherland has never been a real concept. On the contrary, it is a projection of our desires..."

Dina is clearly a figure which fits in the pattern of the so-called diasporic narratives lately considered/adopted by the literary criticism in Macedonia as historically authentic, grounded in the diasporic culture of the Balkans as a region.[2] She moves easily along the liminal spaces of identity and all she does is, in fact, translation. A cross-cultural subject, as she refers to herself, she was used to the postmodern 'otherness' of languages much earlier, in her days of childhood spent in the refugee makeshift houses. So, Dina's geography of desire seems to be conditioned in relation to her sense of an already "translated" woman, if we follow Salman Rushdie's reflection on the etymology of the word. Rushdie's remarks, commented by Homi Bhabha and later by Prof. Harish Trivedi, exploit the meaning of the word *translation* – "to be carried or borne across." As he has been borne across "presumably by an airplane from India and Pakistan to the United Kingdom," (Trivedi 2007) he was a "translated man" but, as Professor Trivedi points out, he neglected to say whether he was at any stage "an original man."

Kica Kolbe also neglects to say whether Dina was ever an original woman. Dina describes herself as an apocryphal Macedonian, as "something", in fact, virtual: "present-day citizen of a former republic of a non-existing state." (Here Kolbe surprisingly disguises a political statement in relation to the mutual necessity for the Macedonians to negotiate over their name, which has become recently a special, if we want to be ironic, 'hermeneutic' question.)

The question of belonging is not determinative for Dina in the first part of the novel. However, the problem of self-identification becomes evident in the second part, where we see her coming back in Skopje, her "city behind the back of Europe." She returns unwillingly, due to some external circumstances, in the febrile atmosphere of a typical post-communist and post-ideological transitional society. Unexpectedly, Dina's fear of coming back in her already provisional home is transformed as she puts her luggage on the floor of her parents' abandoned apartment. This almost archetypal scene is significant for the further development of the novel, because it introduces the turn which is essential not only for its structure, but also for the understanding of the politics of translation in Kolbe's case. From this point on, Kolbe's novel becomes a novel of a quest.

The quest actually begins with the first sensation which strikes Dina's consciousness: it is the scent, the perfume of that 'something' – that 'state of mind' which is conventionally called home. This inexplicable smell, reduced to dried fruits, the smell of the ozone or the smell of Dina's grandmother's humble room ("the scents of disappeared lives") evoke the lost topography of home. The rule of the scent gradually breaks the binary opposition between the centre of the former aesthetic idolatry (Europe) and the chaotic province (Macedonia) and, consequently, the lethal dichotomy of belonging. Here Kolbe deliberately uses a specific word *mirizma (smell)* which is less translatable than the conventional word (*miris*) and, of course, it is not sufficient to say that she evokes Proust's *odeur* or that she, consequently, simply translates (through the act of understanding) Proust's mechanisms of *memoire involontaire*, crucial to his proper quest. What Kolbe does is surely negotiating: by referring to the alleged original (which has, as we all know, a cultural function to drive an idea or set of ideas given a certain form in a particular text) – not in an attempt to speak about things more generally cultural, but in order to produce *a gain* in the process of recontextualization, insisting on the untranslatable nuance/gradation in the word *mirizma*. I am not sure if Kolbe is familiar with Rushdie's novel *Shame* where he, in a certain way, proposes that one should pay attention to the untranslatable words if one wants to understand a culture, but she is certainly familiar with the work of Kundera or Ugrešić, or with Svetlana Boym's remark on the necessity of creating a Dictionary of Untranslatable Terms. Kolbe's persistence on harsh and gentle, rare words confirms these affiliations.

Of course, there is a significant difference between Proust's work and Kolbe's "endeavor" (this word is often used in an ironic mood in the text and it is in relation to Dina's ambition to write "the greatest novel of her time"); while the main character in Proust's quest is the time, the main character in Kolbe's novel is certainly the place: "I am always tracking the past through the nose. I should only reach the place where I can find the true scent (...)" (p.94-5).

Dina "yearns"[3] to organize imaginatively her space as a multiplicity of places/scents in the circumstances where place is principally political. This means that the domestication of space is a problematic process, not only for the virtual refugee as Dina is, but equally for all human beings, especially if we follow Hannah Arendt's remark on refugees as the vanguard of peoples.

The retrieval of the lost topography parallels the retrieval of all "signs" (Deleuze 1964) of Dina's love: love for her old friends, for the fragments of her grandmother's gaze, the forgotten love, David, a Jew of Russian origin, a refugee himself – love being crucial for this reconstruction of the very place/space of her culture. Only when space feels thoroughly familiar to us, says the influential Chinese geographer Yi-Fu Tuan, it has become a *place*. Dina's domestication of space follows the procedures of involuntary memory which brings the imagined place into a state of purity. As Michel de Certeau points out, "places are fragmentary and inward-turning histories, pasts that others are not allowed to read, accumulated times that can be unfolded but like stories held in reverse, remaining in an enigmatic state" (de Certeau 1990).

What Dina does is articulating the topography of remembering, constructing the place imaginatively. Her memorialization of the private histories is crucial for the novel, because the miraculous stories of recovery emphasize the plurality of space/place the narrator inhabits, and at the same time strongly motivate the semantic innovation of language. Dina uses the power of fiction to redescribe another kind of reality, reducing the identity cores to pure fragments of memory, performing different rites around them – and, finally, translating.

In this sense, Kolbe's narrative solutions are a combination of translations: her coined words and expressions evoke, for example, the background of Walter Benjamin's methods of archaeology of the presence (Bojm 2005) as well as his reflections on history ("pearls of crystallized experience" versus irreversibility of time.) Furthermore, Dina's "great novel" which is to be born, in the febrile atmosphere of "Casablanca" (Dina names her fatherland "Casablanca" – a metaphor of her Macedonia and all the small countries which lie at crossroads, the liminal cultures of the "expatriated, exiled and refugees"). It "bears across" the irony and the magic of a modern *bildungsroman*, for instance, Tomas Mann's *Magic Mountain*. The list of her German relatives continues as the stressed lyric dimension, the internalized dialogue and the ethical preoccupations point to Herman Broch and as the utopia of the essayist and mystical dimension of love point to Robert Musil.

Far beyond the issue of translation as a practice of text transfer we are, in fact talking about a whole transcultural practice and in this sense, undoubtedly, Kolbe's novel challenges the boundaries of genre in the Macedonian literary context. She purposefully adopts the patterns of the quest novel from European Modernism, a nostalgic literary convention of a great literary work which strives to give an all-encompassing interpretation of life at a time when the world has already lost its transcendental home. Therefore, the novel is another example of the restitution of the chain world-word-homeland through narration, or another example of Walter Benjamin's concept of translation as a "migrant's dream of survival."

In this case, as in many others, translation as a literary practice includes/activates a specific ethical regime. It can be noticed in the simultaneous identity of the translated text, in the 'and/both' and 'neither/nor' existence of the socially and historically constructed literary world. The idealistic vision of the intercultural encounter, the paradise image of these subtle affiliations hides in itself a kind of doubleness which, in practice fails to justify the pure utopian horizon suggested by the translation theory. The discursive presence of the translated texts, of the 'texts-bridges' (coming from the joint site of the European international community of writers between two coasts) reflects a silent double image, a hidden image of tension between two worlds, as it is most daringly pictured in one of Franz Kafka's shortest stories, *The Bridge*. In it, Kafka describes a man who was a bridge:

> I was stiff and cold, I was a bridge, I lay over a ravine. My toes on one side, my fingers clutching the other, I had clamped myself fast into the crumbling clay. The tails of my coat fluttered at my sides. Far below brawled the icy trout stream. No tourist strayed to this impassable height, the bridge was not yet traced on any map. So I lay and waited; I could only wait. Without falling, no bridge, once spanned, can cease to be a bridge (p.372).

With his hands on one side of a steep chasm and his feet on the other, he lay waiting to carry travelers safely across a river and the sharp rocks below. As a traveler stepped onto the bridge, it caused such pain that the bridge turned around to see what the traveler was doing to hurt him.

> But then – I was just following him in thought over mountain and valley – he jumped with both feet on the middle of my body. I shuddered with wild pain, not knowing what was happening. Who was it? A child? A dream? A wayfarer? A suicide? A tempter? A destroyer? And I turned so as to see him. A bridge to turn around! I had not yet turned quiet around when I already began to fall, I fell and in a moment I was torn and transpierced by the sharp rocks which had always gazed up at me so peacefully from the rushing water (p.372).

Did Kafka, as a special case of 'diasporic' writer, as another 'translated man', felt the responsibility to "support unsteady travelers" and to provide passage between cultures, between languages? Did he feel, as a bridge, the weight of responsibility not to turn around, the burden to out-maneuver the master discourses of power? Did he really articulate the curse of the two shores, the two commitments, the possibility of never crossing over?

It is often said that literature, culture, translation itself are a bridge between civilizations, but the bridge itself has something to say in this Kafkian vision: its own fear, the isthmus between life and what is not yet, or no longer – life. The bridge, as an image, contains the counter-narrative of the utopian trajectory of the translation theory, or, in Jan Patocka's words, the problematicity of living in amplitude, the problematicity of the plurality of place, in fact, the problematicity of the placeless place.

Notes
[1] Kica Kolbe lives and works in Langenfeld, Germany since 1985.
[2] To lay a claim to the 'historical authenticity' of the diasporic narratives is a very problematic position and, clearly, not very logical.
[3] Kolbe uses the word *yearning*, an equivalent of the word 'kopnež' in the Macedonian language, something between desire and nostalgia

Bibliography
Agamben, Giorgio. 2000. *Means without Ends: Notes on Politics.* Minneapolis: University of Minnesota Press.
Certeau, Michel de. 1990. *L'invention du cotidien.* Paris: Gallimard.
Bojm, Svetlana. 2005. *Budućnost nostalgije.* Beograd: Geopoetika.
Burke, Peter. 2005/6. *Lost (and Found) in Translation: A Cultural History of Translators and Translating in Early Modern Europe.* Wassenaar: NIAS.
Deleuze, Gilles. 1964. *Proust et les signes.* Paris: Seuil.
Kafka, Franz. 1983. *The Bridge* (tr. Willa and Edwin Muir). New York: Schocken books.
Kelly, Stephen. 2007. 'The Island that is Nowhere: Or, Cultural Translation, an Utopian Project?' in Kelly, Stephen and Johnston, David (eds) *Betwixt and Between: Place and Cultural Translation.* Cambridge: Cambridge Scholars Publishing.
Kolbe, Kica B. 1999. *Egejci.* Skopje: Kultura.
Trivedi, Harish. 2007. *Translating Culture vs. Cultural Translation.* Online at: http://www.uiowa.edu/~iwp/91st/91st_Archive/vol4_n1/pdfs/trivedi.pdf (Consulted at 25/01/09).

`

Translating Dubravka Ugrešić and David Albahari

Ellen Elias-Bursać

Abstract: Dubravka Ugrešić and David Albahari share a generational postmodern aesthetic, but they have embraced these artistic challenges differently. Ugrešić is outward-facing, employs narrative rooted in folk literature, and her voice is wry, personal and outspokenly critical; Albahari's voice is darkly humorous, aloof, and his writing is introverted, experimental. When faced with the artistic issues arising from the wars of the 1990s, Ugrešić first turned to essay and later returned to fiction, while Albahari stayed with fiction, moving from short stories to shorter and longer novels, at a time when both of them were taking up domicile abroad, Ugrešić in the Netherlands, Albahari in Canada. During and after the wars of the 90s, they used the poetic they had each developed in the pre-war period to address the wounds of war, loss and dislocation. Both writers have stayed in touch with domestic audiences while being widely translated and read abroad.
Keywords: David Albahari, Dubravka Ugrešić, postmodernism, translation, war trauma, displacement, exile, transnational fiction, Croatian literature, Serbian literature, literature of the former Yugoslavia

Dubravka Ugrešić and I met in Zagreb in the 1970s when we were part of the same circle of friends and both involved in Slavic Studies. I was living as an American in Yugoslavia at the time, studying literature and working as a translator. We were friends for many years before I translated a book of hers. David Albahari and I, on the other hand, met much later, just before the war, in Belgrade, in the context of my interest in translating his short stories, and our acquaintance has revolved around our work together as translator and author ever since. I have always in my own mind been comparing the novels and short stories of these two writers ever since I began reading them, partly because they and I are close in age and share a generational literary aesthetic, and partly because my life, with its 18 years in Zagreb, mirrors in reverse their lives with 15 years each living abroad, just as my English translations mirror their writing in Croatian and Serbian.

A reader picking up a text by Dubravka Ugrešić and comparing it to a text by David Albahari will be more impressed by the differences in

their writing than their similarities. Where Albahari has concentrated
on form, Ugrešić has been more compelled by substance. While she is
outward-facing, often employing narrative rooted in folk and fairy
tale, he is introverted, experimental, modern. Where Ugrešić's writing
is personal, wry, and, after the outbreak of war, outspokenly critical,
Albahari's is darkly humorous, even maniacal at times, and aloof.

Yet the two writers have much in common. They are the same age,
started writing at the same time, and both were innovators in their
exploration of the possibilities offered by metafiction. They have each
published roughly the same number of books touching on the same
genres – novels, short stories, children's books and essays – and both
are the most prominent writers of their generation in the Croatian and
Serbian circles of what used to be Yugoslavia. They have both lived
abroad since about 1993 in voluntary exile, David Albahari in
Calgary, Dubravka Ugrešić in Amsterdam, and they have both
written, among other things, on displacement, exile and the trauma of
war.

Before the war David Albahari and Dubravka Ugrešić are fascinated
by playfulness, intertextuality, quotation, self-referentiality in their
writing. Albahari published his first book of short stories in 1973,
Ugrešić hers in 1979.

Take, for instance, the opening paragraphs of their best known
pre-war stories, for Ugrešić: *A Hot Dog in a Warm Bun*, for Albahari:
My Wife Has Light Eyes.

Ugrešić's story is a satirical latter-day Gogol's 'Nose' situated in
modern Zagreb. The story opens with the protagonist, Dr. Nada Matić,
setting off into the city one day on her way to work:

> On the twenty-fifth of March a truly unbelievable thing took place in Zagreb.
> Nada Matić, a young doctor specializing in plastic surgery, awoke in her room
> and looked at the clock. It was 6:15. Nada jumped out of bed, jumped into the
> shower, squatted under the stream of water, then, lighting a cigarette, jumped into
> a terry cloth robe. It was 6:25. She pulled on her gray spring suit, daubed some
> rouge on her cheeks, and grabbed her bag. It was 6:30. She locked the door,
> finished the cigarette in the elevator, and hurried off to catch her train.
>   By the time Nada Matić stepped off the train, it was 6:50. And just then,
> right in the middle of the square, Nada Matić was overcome by a sudden,
> unusually intense hunger. She rushed over to the Skyscraper Cafeteria, which
> served hot dogs in warm buns, nervously calling out to the waitress, "More
> mustard, please!" greedily grabbed the hot dog, and impatiently threw away the
> napkin. (That is what Nada Matić did. That is what I do too: I always dispose of

those unnecessary and shamefully tiny scraps of paper waitresses use for wrapping hot dogs.)

Then she set off across the square. She was about to bring the hot dog to her lips, when – was it some dark sense of foreboding or a ray of the March morning sun alighting on the object in question, illuminating it with its own special radiance? In either case and to make a long story short, she glanced down at the fresh pink hot dog and her face convulsed in horror. For what did she see peering through the longish bun and ocherish mustard foam but a genuine, bona fide...! Nada came to a complete and utter halt. No, there could be no doubt. "Glans, corpus, radix, corpora cavernosa, corpora spongiosa, praeputium, frenulum, scrotum," our heroine Nada Matić, thought, running through her totally useless anatomy class knowledge and still not believing her eyes. No, that thing in the bun was most definitely not a hot dog!" (Ugrešić 2005: 107-108)

Albahari's story, set in a non-specific Serbian urban environment, is a bickering exchange between husband and wife over the nature of fiction and literary theory that mirrors their relationship. The bickering relationship is a power struggle between the wife, defending the integrity of art, and the husband, the narrator, who relativizes whatever the wife says with the power that his first-person perspective gives him.

"This will be a simple story," I think, "and it will have no compound sentences."

"Don't be silly," says my wife. "That sentence is already pretty compound."

I turn and look at her. I see her as I've never seen her before, but she doesn't know it. "What are you," I say, "a mind reader?"

My wife doesn't answer. This is one of her talents. Instead she says something else. "If you have lied to the reader in your very first sentence, how can you expect your reader to believe your next one?"

I stare at the blank sheet of paper in front of me. "I didn't lie to my reader," I say, "because I haven't written anything down yet."

"But you thought it," says my wife.

This resembles one of those exhausting marital spats from the stories and novels of John Updike. I have no time for that. So I don't beat around the bush. "According to you," I say to my wife as if she'd written the gospel, "according to you," I repeat for the sake of inner rhythm, "prose is supposed to be truthful."

"Are you asking or declaring?" asks my wife.

"Asking."

"Declaring," she says. (Albahari 1996:119)

In these passages Dubravka Ugrešić and David Albahari make reference to other literatures: Ugrešić to Gogol and Albahari to Updike. Indeed the international dimension has been essential to both of them from the start. With Ugrešić it was familial ties to Bulgaria, her study of Russian literature, and her translations of writers such as Daniil Harms and Boris Pilnyak. With Albahari, his international reference point was Israel, rock and roll, and his translations of American writers such as Robert Coover, John Barth and Thomas Pynchon. This predisposition may well have contributed to their abiding interests, both through writing and translation: their personal trajectory from the former Yugoslavia to life elsewhere, their own literary translations and their involvement in the translation of their work into other languages. They have both maintained a pronounced international approach throughout – working closely with their translators, speaking and teaching all over Europe and North America. Indeed it was the fact that both of them had been invited abroad in the early 1990s, Dubravka Ugrešić to Amsterdam and David Albahari to Calgary, that gave each the basis on which to make the decision to stay abroad.

When the war began both Ugrešić and Albahari published works with which to mark their break with their literary communities, airing their personal trauma, and their resolve to step away: Ugrešić with her book of essays *Have a Nice Day,* and Albahari with his story *The Cloak.*

David Albahari has said of *The Cloak* that it represented his divorce from the Serbian literature of the time. It starts, much as 'My Wife Has Light Eyes' starts, with a bickering exchange between a husband and a wife:

> "You don't write stories about me anymore," my wife says sadly.
> I look at her; everything has left its mark: the children, illness, life, war, death.
> "I don't tell stories anymore," I say.
> The sentence doesn't comfort her. (Albahari 1996: 154)

In *Have A Nice Day* Dubravka Ugrešić makes a more dramatic departure not only from wartime Croatia but her writing up until that point, by venturing into a particular form of the essay:

> This is an indecent book. I have always believed (and I still do) that a writer with any self-respect should avoid three things:
>   a) autobiography
>   b) writing about other countries
>   c) diaries
> All three smack of narcissism, which is undoubtedly the basic premise of any literary act, but ought not also to be its outcome. And in all three genres this outcome is hard to avoid. [...]

So this book has been written against my personal and literary convictions. But excuses, of whatever kind, are always superfluous: this book belongs to genres a) and b) and c). This book is neither a) nor b) nor c). It was meant to be a book about one thing, it turned out to be a book about something else, and written for someone quite different. Even its author is uncertain. (Ugrešić 1995: 11-12)

With these passages both authors step into the war zone in their art, while both still holding firm to the postmodern toolset they chose from the start, the key difference being that while Albahari sticks to fiction, building on his 'my wife' theme and his competing voices, Ugrešić inaugurates her special brand of essay, an in-between genre, peppered with juxtapositions, intertextual references to other literatures and film, anecdote, social commentary, and commentary on the war; the stories and anecdotes she uses to make her point take her essays to the brink of fiction.

In retrospect, it is apparent that for both of these writers, this moment was not so much a divorce as a reformulation. David Albahari and Dubravka Ugrešić have stayed a vital part of both Serbian and Croatian literatures, probably more so than either of them could have imagined in the early 1990s. Albahari was the first Serbian writer to be published in Croatia after the war, and Ugrešić published a collection of her novels and short stories in both Belgrade and Zagreb in 2001–2002, and has since then continued to publish each of her new books in both Zagreb and Belgrade.

Living abroad, both Dubravka Ugrešić and David Albahari addressed the question of war trauma in their writing. In the book of essays *The Culture of Lies*, her novels *Museum of Unconditional Surrender* and *Ministry of Pain* and in her recent book of essays *Nobody's Home,* Dubravka Ugrešić broadens the theme of displacement and exile, reaching ultimately for a global perspective, with the suggestion that displacement is currently the world's, or certainly Europe's, central condition. Her most recent novel *Baba Yaga Laid an Egg* is about many things, but among them it takes this exploration of exile to the internal isolation experienced by the elderly in society, particularly elderly women.

In the early years of the war David Albahari moves from short stories to short novels and devotes his wartime trilogy: *Bait, Snow Man, Svetski putnik (World Traveler)* to an expatriate protagonist. The protoganist of each of the three is a writer who has left Serbia to live in Canada – *Snow Man* being his ultimate exploration of both loss and exile: no place or person in the novel has a name except a dog named Fredi. Even his postwar novel *Leeches*[1], while it is told in flashbacks of life in Belgrade and neighboring Zemun, is narrated by a writer in self-exile reminiscing on the events that led him to flee Belgrade to escape persecution. Of Albahari's writing after 1993, only *Götz & Meyer* and *Ludvig*, at the time of the writing of this article, have been about a protagonist who actually lives from start to finish in Serbia.

When Dubravka Ugrešić and David Albahari first began publishing their work in the 1970s they were making their debut in the larger context of the literatures of Slovenia, Serbia and Croatia, which were principally engaged at the time with the artistic challenge of spotlighting a nation-specific history, discarding the larger culture of Yugoslavia, and celebrating the demise of socialism. These were subjects which held little appeal for Ugrešić and Albahari, who belonged to the first generation born and educated after World War II and who had benefited from the best that Yugoslav socialism had to offer. In the 1980s while other writers were publishing run-away bestsellers which pulled back the curtains to expose the secrets and scandals of Tito's Yugoslavia, Dubravka Ugrešić and David Albahari were writing funny or poignant stories about urban life devoid of most Yugoslav-specific cultural reference. With the advent of the war those writers who had devoted themselves to the blazing national issues spent themselves in the larger conflagration. Few of them are writing still today and those who are still writing no longer command the bestseller status and the currency they enjoyed in the 1980s. Meanwhile, ironically, Ugrešić and Albahari had the breadth of audience, the personal commitment to a non-nationalist perspective, and the freedom that living abroad gave them to address the subject of the trauma of the war for all its victims. Who could have predicted ten years before that these two postmodern fans of wry, cosmopolitan humor, metafiction and intertextuality would be the voices best suited to address the wounds of war, loss and dislocation, yet it was precisely their anti-nationalist sentiments and universalist poetic that allowed them to do so.

I would say that the fact that both these writers make particular use of *mother* and *father* characters in their writing is directly related to their choice of transnational fiction. David Albahari's expatriate novels use the protagonist's mother and father as the anchors for his characters' otherwise unanchored existence. Dubravka Ugrešić also uses the protagonist's mother, particularly in *Museum of Unconditional Surrender* and *Baba Yaga Laid an Egg,* to define home. In doing so the family members who figure large in their writing replace membership in the community, which their characters, and they as writers, left. I suggest this because the characters of *mother* and *father* in Albahari's writing and the character of *mother* in Ugrešić's writing are accorded the same status as absolutes that the 'nation' is accorded in the work of the national writers – never questioned, never ironicized, treated as a given.

The same could be said of the attention both these writers pay to layout and design in their published work, the visual experience of the text serving as yet another anchor, making the visual experience of the text part of its sense of place. Albahari's preference is the rigor imposed by his use of no indentation of paragraphs. He has explained this choice as follows:

> Today a novelist writes for a select group of readers, and if there is anything that compels him, it is the pressure to offer as demanding a work as possible. [...] The reading of a novel is its creation, and therein lies my conviction that there is no point in coddling a reader. The reader should bring to the reading of the novel the same measure of effort that the novelist brought to its writing; the labyrinthine structure of the novels typical of postmodern prose is best suited to an interactive relationship like this. Hence my decision to write in long paragraphs, for a novel written in one or several long paragraphs is actually a labyrinth or, better yet, a quicksand mire of a dense text which will quickly engulf the indecisive reader. (Albahari 2007a: 4)

Ugrešić feels equally strongly that her writing should be laid out in a way that enhances what she has to say, but her preference moves in the opposite direction. By using paragraph breaks, indentation, and extra spacing to cluster her ideas together she works to make the texts appealing and readable. I offer the layout of this article as an example of her style. Each new cluster begins with an unindented paragraph and is separated from other paragraph clusters by extra spacing. While Albahari's essential expressive unit is the sentence, Ugrešić's is the paragraph.

Worlds and cultures face-to-face, the dynamics of displacement and encounter, play a central role in Dubravka Ugrešić's writing; her essays are interwoven with poetic, human moments such this one in a New York pedicure salon in *USA Nails*:

> I was the last customer. I entertained myself by watching how the Vietnamese proprietor was teaching a young Mexican woman with plump fingers how to groom nails. The Vietnamese man was gentle and patient. First he applied polish to the nails on her hand, demonstrating how to brush the surface of the nail properly. Then he stretched his own hand out to her so she could demonstrate what she had learned. They made a perfect picture. Lit by light from the street, the teacher and pupil polishing each others' nails was a scene worthy of Vermeer. (Ugrešić 2008: 133)

But also typical of Ugrešić's essays is the acerbic voice of the cultural critic, such as in this passage in *Transition: Morphs & Sliders & Polymorphs*, lambasting public intellectuals who prop themselves up in war and post-war on the crutch of postmodernist rhetoric:

> The public intellectual is extinct, but his craft—providing intellectual services— still flourishes. Here is the paradox: the more disgraceful the moral death of the intellectual, the more urgent the need for his services. As far as ex-Yugoslavs are concerned, those who were card-carrying members of the party immediately rushed to support their nationalist leaders Tuđman and Milosević. Their leaders, after all, were themselves converted communists. Those same intellectuals today—if they have survived—are the most passionate supporters of post-postmodernism, the ideology of cynicism, games (Ah, everything is just a game!) and image (This isn't my real identity, it is merely one of my public personas!), the carnivalizing of ideology and politics (Everything is a carnival, and I am part of it!), and marketing strategies (This is my marketing strategy, not what I think!). Those who are pushing anti-nationalism today (Why, after all, everyone knows that national identity is nothing more than a construct!) were cheering as the boys went off to battle a dozen years ago—the Serbs seeing off the Serbian soldiers, and the Croats seeing off their own, Croatian troops—to slaughter each other. Today's passionate propagators of the theory of simulacrum, virtuality, and multiple identities (I feel fine in any one of them!) are mainly those intellectuals who use postmodern theory (Poor old Baudriallard!) as an alibi for themselves and others for the practice of moral conversion. If we proclaim that everything is a game, we cease to be responsible. We become children. (Ugrešić 2008: 173)

Albahari has used his poetic of bickering voices to bring the focus to relativization. There is a moment in *Leeches* when the protagonist, fleeing his pursuers, ducks in among some buildings and finds himself in a children's playground, on a swing:

> The seat of the swing cut into my legs, the moon slid back and forth above me, or maybe it was me sliding back and forth beneath it, who could say, everything is relative in this world anyway, especially when a person is swinging with his head flung back, with the blood rushing to the brain, prompting him to think things he might never otherwise think... (Albahari 2005: 212-273)

This commitment to relativism underlies everything that Albahari writes, even when he allows his protagonist a view on politics and a degree of heroism as he does in *Leeches*.

Humor holds a central place in the stories and novels of both David Albahari and Dubravka Ugrešić, though while Ugrešić's sense of humor is wry, Albahari's is sardonic.

This example of Ugrešić's humor is taken from a scene in her latest novel, *Baba Yaga Laid an Egg*, when the protagonist's mother, a woman obsessed by cleanliness, is being rushed to the hospital:

> Over the last three years we have often had to call an ambulance. It is the easiest and quickest way to sidestep the elaborate bureaucratic procedures and get my mother admitted immediately to hospital. We called an ambulance once when she was in a crisis. As the nurses, supporting her under the arms, were guiding her to the lift, Mum ducked down, spryly, and snatched up the plastic rubbish bag by the door, left there to be taken down and tossed into the bin.
> "Ma'am, please...!" shrieked the doctor, catching sight of her. (Ugrešić 2009: 24)

In contrast, this passage from Albahari's novel *Leeches* flips neo-fascist attack to grim hilarity with a description of the moment when a pile of excrement is left in front of the protagonist's door:

> One night, on the doormat in front of my door I found a little mound of excrement. I bent over, then kneeled down, in order to examine it more closely. It was firm, compact, and I could just picture the effort with which the person had squeezed it out. Perhaps the squeezing was even accompanied by pain, the rupturing of a blood vessel along the rim of the anus, but the light in the stairwell was too weak for me to be able to spot any traces of coagulated blood. Judging by the position of the stool, tidily coiled, the person had produced it while crouching over the doormat and someone else, I assume, was keeping watch at the front door to the building. If they had brought it there from somewhere else, surely the natural snake-like appearance would have been spoiled, at least smeared... (Albahari 2005: 82)

Speaking as someone who has translated books by both these writers, I can say that they are very different to translate. I have been translating David Albahari's writing since the 1990s (*Words Are Something Else, Snow Man, Götz & Meyer,* and now *Leeches*) and have more recently translated Dubravka Ugrešić's *Nobody's Home* as well as Part I of *Baba Yaga.* Making the first draft of a translation of David Albahari's writing is deceptively easy. His language is spare, his vocabulary simple. But if his sentence is translated literally into English the resulting translation is a flat, static text with none of the power and poetry that the original somehow tucks in between the words. Once the first draft is done it takes many re-readings to tighten the language gradually in little edits. The tighter and more powerful the text becomes, the more lucid it is, and Albahari's lucidity is his finest quality. Albahari is focused first and foremost on form, his sentence, as his comments above would suggest. The challenge to the translator is to translate the sentence as closely as possible while keeping the sense crystal clear. Here is an example where Albahari ironicizes his own meandering sentence:

> "Fine," said Marko, explaining that he had come to show me something, or to take me somewhere where he'd show me something, something which, he felt, I had to see, because it was directly related, whatever it was, or at least that was how he perceived it, to things that had been going on with me recently, which I would be able to see for myself, and even if he had read it wrong, which was not impossible, it is human, after all, to err, but even in that case, he said, I'd be interested in what he had to show me, and we should get going as soon as possible, he got up, which was a lucky thing because tangled sentences like this one were terribly draining for him. (Albahari 2005: 148)

Ugrešić's writing, on the other hand, is all about substance. She has ideas, images, sequences she means to get across, and she is not wedded to any one feature of the original punctuation, image, or sequence structure at the cost of obscuring what she has to say. She is not averse to allowing a translator to add cultural references that were not on the original, such as this passage from 'A Postcard from my Vacation':

> The tycoons wrangle like village dogs over what is left of the old communist workers' vacation centers (to eradicate the last traces of that "grim communist past," when workers were able to afford a vacation on the coast). There aren't any Serbs left, and that, too, is auspicious: their summer homes, with which they had "occupied" the Croatian coast, have long since been blown up, squatted in, or snapped up for a song—with offers the previous owners could not refuse—by the local inhabitants. Others are summering on the Adriatic now, the more "stable"

guests: the English, Austrians, Germans, Italians, and the more generously solvent Russians. (Ugrešić 2008: 274)

The phrase "with offers the previous owners could not refuse" with its oblique reference to the film *The Godfather* (a neutral translation without the addition of the reference to *The Godfather* would have been: "...purchased by forced for niggling sums from the previous owners") was an addition to the essay. Such references work well in translations of Ugrešić's writing, which is already so full of intertextual referentiality.

Dubravka Ugrešić values playfulness above all else in a translator and an ear for the lively intertextuality that peppers her writing and creates the underpinnings for her intellectual universe of Slavic, European, and American cultural reference. The other challenge in translating writing that is as anecdotal and pithy as are Ugrešić's essays, is to give her translation life while steering clear of the catchy sound-bite style of Madison Avenue. The complex nuances of Ugrešić's essays must not be undercut by letting the language slip too far in this direction.

In terms of how each of them has been received by their Croatian and Serbian readers, respectively, Dubravka Ugrešić, with her preference for the essay, chose a form of direct authorial address. The essays that she wrote at the start of the war, sharply critical of the harnessing of literature and culture to the nationalist cause, made her a scapegoat in public life in Croatia. Her books sell well there and she is very popular with her Croatian readers but her popularity is not reflected in her critical reception in Croatia, which has been colored by the controversies she has stirred over the years, and this is still the case in 2008, though her work is no longer perceived to be quite as acerbic or controversial as it was ten-fifteen years ago.

David Albahari, with his insistence on prose based on the interplay of two voices, has been invested in developing a multivalent fictional approach, and generally, with the exception of his novel *Leeches*, he has written not so much about the war as about the loss and displacement the war caused. Though he lives in Calgary, he has been back to Belgrade every year for the October Book Fair, and has used this regular involvement at the Fair to maintain a strong presence in Belgrade literary life. He has been emulated by the young writers and embraced by the establishment as an essential part of Serbian culture and is perceived as the leading writer of his generation.

Each of these writers is now following a distinct trajectory. Dubravka Ugrešić wrote two novels and several books of short stories before 1988, and then gave herself over to essay writing for ten years, returning to fiction only with *Museum of Unconditional Surrender* in 1998. While *Museum* is situated in Berlin, a book of photographs, and wartime Zagreb, *Ministry of Pain* takes place in Amsterdam, with the ghost of the former Yugoslavia always there in tandem. Unlike these two works, steeped in the experience of living displaced in Western Europe, the newest novel, *Baba Yaga Laid an Egg* starts in the Zagreb of today, then moves to a spa in the Czech Republic, and then to Bulgaria, with a memorable gem-like description of the trauma of post-war life in Zagreb in this passage:

> Her pension was barely enough to cover her basic outgoings and food, while her meagre savings had vanished with the Ljubljana Bank some fifteen years before, when the country fell apart and suddenly her bank was in a different state, and everyone had been rushing headlong to steal from everyone else. Had she wanted, she could have derived some bitter satisfaction from it all: in comparison with many other people's losses her were negligible, because she had simply had nothing in the first place.
>
> Then all at once, everything had turned ugly. The people around her had grown ugly with hatred, and then with self-pity and the realization that they had been cheated. They had all developed a rat-like expression, even the young, those who had begun to come of age breathing in their parents' poisonous breath.
>
> Beba was weeping because she could not remember when she had last had a holiday. She used to go in both summer and winter. Winter holidays on the coast had been especially cheap. Now they were out of the question, now everything was out of the question. The coast had apparently been bought up by wealthy foreigners and local tycoons. (Ugrešić 2009: 88-89)

This succinct summary of war-related trauma functions, within Ugrešić's larger opus, as a post-war nod to her wartime writing and a signal that she is exploring new subjects, such as, in *Baba Yaga*, folklore and the Slavic cultural context. Hence, even in her return to Zagreb she is suggesting a broader Slavic perspective.

After his attention to Jewish themes, the 'my wife' stories, and the stories of life spent moving between countries and continents, David Albahari returns to Zemun and Belgrade in *Götz & Meyer, Leeches,* and *Ludvig* and has embarked on an exploration of writing about history from a postmodern perspective. In *Ludvig* Belgrade actually figures as something of a protagonist. Albahari's experience of the significance of Belgrade as a place has clearly been shaped by the time he has spent living away:

> So it is with Belgrade: if you stay there, you'll be sorry, but if you leave it, you will also be sorry. No one who has ever lived in Belgrade can leave it. Anyone who tries to go, soon will discover he has only crept into Belgrade even more, like those bugs which get under the bark of a tree, except it is the bugs destroying the tree, feeding on its sap, while those who get under the skin, so to say, of Belgrade, become Belgrade's food and feel as if the city is sapping their vital fluids, until all that is left of those people is a shell, a fragile skeleton barely able to move, forever losing its balance. Belgrade is, in fact, a cannibal city... (Albahari 2007b: 156–157)

Of David Albahari's novels, only *Leeches* speaks directly of the war. While still structured around the bickering relationship of two characters, in this case close friends, the novel introduces a heroic protagonist and evokes the deadly atmosphere of Belgrade in 1998, just before the bombing in the spring of 1999, with the difference that the protagonist's alter ego, his friend Marko, no longer wields the moral superiority that the 'wife' had in Albahari's earlier writing, ultimately turning out to be one of the villains, while the authorial power that Albahari's earlier first-person protagonist enjoyed finds expression here in the protagonist's decision to resort to silence.

Even before the war both David Albahari and Dubravka Ugrešić create an urban setting for their prose which is essentially universalist. Though they call it Zagreb, or Belgrade, or Zemun, it could be any city anywhere, just as their characters could be urbanites anywhere. They sidestep the exclusivist nationalist poetics of the 1980s to speak to an inclusive audience that spans the entire Yugoslav readership, and when that readership collapses with the outbreak of war and they move abroad, they both expand their reach, through translations of their work and their presence in Europe and North America at conferences and universities, to readers throughout the Western world. Precisely because of this reach they are able to and committed to addressing the trauma of the war by writing about exile and loss, though in very different ways. Since the war they have both moved beyond war themes to explore new narrative forms and subjects – Ugrešić looking at Slavic culture as the flip side of Europe, Albahari engaged in exploring a postmodern approach to history, while never losing sight of the dimension that the war brought to their work.

They both rely on humor to propel them through the often ticklish, painful topics they take on, and they have held on throughout to their post-modern devices of intertextuality, quotation, metafiction.

They both decided to divorce themselves from the nationalist literature of the war period and forge their own way as writers, to take on the themes of exile and displacement. Each has made his or her way back to their domestic readership, Dubravka Ugrešić in Croatia and David Albahari in Serbia, while still keeping in touch with readers living in the other Yugoslav successor states. They have also built up strong followings in other countries where almost all their work has been translated: Ugrešić is most widely read in Polish, German, Dutch and English, while Albahari is well-translated into Hebrew, German, French and English. The futures of these two prolific writers promise to diverge even more over time, now that they are moving beyond the artistic challenges thrust upon them by the war and their own displacement, yet they will probably always be similar in their dissimilarity.

Notes
[1] As this article goes to press, Leeches, the English translation of Albahari's novel *Pijavice*, is forthcoming with Houghton Mifflin. The passages quoted from Leeches are taken from the manuscript of Ellen Elias-Bursać's English translation; the page numbers given here for quotations are cited from the Serbian original.

Bibliography
Albahari, David. 1996. *Words Are Something Else* (tr. E. Elias-Bursać). Evanston IL: Northwestern University Press.
— 2001. *Bait* (tr. S. Agnone). Evanston IL: Northwestern University Press.
— 2004. *Svetski putnik*. Belgrade: Stubovi kulture.
— 2005. *Pijavice*. Belgrade: Stubovi kulture.
— 2005a. *Snow Man* (tr. E. Elias-Bursać). Toronto: Douglas & McIntyre.
— 2005b. *Götz & Meyer* (tr. E. Elias-Bursać). New York NY: Harcourt Brace.
— 2007a. 'The Novel and History'. Presented at the *International Forum on the Novel* (Lyons, June 2007). Published in French translation by Editions Christian Bourgois; cited here from unpublished English translation.
— 2007b. *Ludvig*. Belgrade: Stubovi kulture.
Ugrešić, Dubravka. 1995. *Have a Nice Day: from the Balkan War to the American Dream* (tr. C. Hawkesworth). New York NY: Viking.
— 1998. *The Culture of Lies: Antipolitical Essays* (tr. C. Hawkesworth). University Park PA: Pennsylvania State University Press.

— 2002. *Museum of Unconditional Surrender* (tr. C. Hawkesworth). New York NY: New Directions Press.

— 2005. 'A Hot Dog in a Warm Bun' (tr. M.H. Heim) in Ugrešić, Dubravka, *Lend Me Your Character*. Normal IL: Dalkey Archive Press: 107–127.

— 2007. *Ministry of Pain* (tr. M.H. Heim). New York NY: Harper Perennial Press.

— 2008. *Nobody's Home* (tr. E. Elias-Bursać). Rochester NY: Open Letter Press.

— 2009. *Baba Yaga Laid an Egg* (tr. E. Elias-Bursać, C. Hawkesworth & M. Thompson). Edinburgh & London: Canongate.

Exile or Exodus:
D. Ugrešić's *The Museum of Unconditional Surrender* and Iliya Troyanov's *The World Is Big and Salvation Lurks around the Corner*

Dimitar Kambourov

Abstract: The text attempts to offer a theoretical formulae of literature of exile by comparing two exemplary novels in the field: Ugrešić's *The Museum of Unconditional Surrender* and Troyanov's *The World is Big and Salvation Lurks around the Corner*. By overcoming their close reading the text comes to the idea of separating exile and nostalgia through a theory of love indifferent humility towards the world as an always already alien and lost home.
Keywords: emigrant literature, exile, nostalgia, memory, globalisation.

> *...Питам те*
> *защо рисуваш в моите тракийски къщи*
> *танцувачи на фламенко. ...*
> *Питам те,*
> *защо рисуваш белите немкини в черно...*
> *Питам те,*
> *защо рисуваш кипариси и маслини*
> *до брезите на Русия? ...*
> *ти на всяка чужда гара*
> *слизаш в своята Испания, ...*
> *ти рисуваш по земята*
> *само своята Испания.*
> (Hanchev, V. 1966: 182–184)

> *It was about that time that my life radically changed, I was living in exile, or whatever it's called. I was changing countries like shoes. I was performing that fall-of-the-Wall item in my own life... With time I acquired an enviable elasticity. ... Those little, firm facts, stamps in our passport, accumulate and at certain moment they become illegible lines. They suddenly begin to trace an inner map, the map of the unreal, the imaginary. And it is only then that they express the immeasurable experience of exile. Yes, exile is like a nightmare ... it seems to us that we have already been there...* (Dubravka Ugrešić 1997: 118–9)

A Bulgarian joke from the communist period, unsure of whether it should stay in the realm of philosophy or venture into politics, goes: A man is at the tailor's to have a suit made. The tailor says: "Come tomorrow, the suit will be ready, no need of fitting." The man comes in on the next day and the suit is ready, only when he tries it on, it looks terrible: the one sleeve is longer than the other, one of the creases goes astray, the left shoulder is higher, the right one hangs. "What is this?" asks the man. "Don't worry, everything will be fine, could you raise a little the right shoulder and drop the left, now turn this leg inside and stretch this arm, well, you see now how beautifully it fits you and suits you!" The man then walks along the street in his new suit and with his new gait and hears someone sharing with his companions: "Look, what a freak yet how beautifully his suit suits him!"

The following joke is about a man who has been caught as he was trying to cross the border, all dressed in white. "Hey, stupid, where are you off to with this white suit on?" asks the guard. The man starts brushing his suit and murmurs: "Where on Earth am I heading for with this white suit on?"

The issue of the recently flourishing literature written by migrants, exiles or trans-national nomads seems to be well covered by these jokes. Once it has been abandoned, the motherland is bound to remain both an object of disgust and of desire; the better the new identity suits the worse it fits – as if a well-made suit on a freak not aware of where he is going. The question is what makes this sort of literature indispensable today.[1] If these were the quantitative data on the size of print runs, the number of awards and the general perception of freshness and vitality imported – or smuggled – into the somewhat stuffy atmosphere of contemporary western literature(s), it would be rather a question of literary history and cultural analysis.[2]

If it is the next 'latest thing', it should probably be contextualized through concepts like globalization, free flow of people, goods and services, exoticism, book market, publishing empires, bored or borrowed critics, etc. Then it would not require a theoretical apparatus tailored expressly for it, as the post-structuralist post-modern ready-made 'difference' would do. Indeed, the recent theoretical and artistic reflections on the phenomenon imply such sufficiency. Twenty or so years after Deleuse and Guattari's "Toward a Minor Literature" there is not much new work done on approaching theoretically the issue of today's cross-border, trans-national, immigrant, diasporic or exilic literature and art.[3] The questions of memory and writing outside the nation have been addressed in various ways.[4] The concepts of in-betweenness, hybridity and creolisation have been put at work and a kind of theoretical appendix has been supplemented to the already established theoretical difference readapted to serve another identity project.[5]

Since the tendency seems irreversible, the question is whether there are theoretical gains to be made out of it or does exilic literature rather lead to a theoretical predicament? If modern writers are exiles *per se,* predestined to make neither prophet nor profit in their home countries, does it really make any difference whether they write 'home' or 'abroad'? Is not their work then but another agency challenging the very notions of 'home' and 'abroad'? If we agree with Kristeva that the modern writer is predestined to be cosmopolitan, then either the exiled writers simply share all too literally the fate of the essential writers-exiles or such literalness naturalizes the common status of today's writer.[6] Is not the writer of modernity deterritorialised by definition through the literal and metaphorical power of so radically temporal an adjective as 'modern'? Or is it that in cases of exile and immigration, theory once again exposes the unique personal experiences as a universal metaphor, thus blurring the differences and burying the singularity?

The recent interest in the literature of exile might have the ingenious design to provide a biographical, existential, or natural motivation for writing that goes beyond any natural, mimetic or psychological impulse. Such motivation would again have a structurally taming effect, though.

Is it possible, then, to tackle the literature of exile in a non-domesticating way? Could we conceive of a theory of exile writing that goes beyond its reading as another reincarnation of the postmodern idiom, only this time naturalized and morally justified? Since the issue of literary exiles and immigrations is gaining currency, perhaps it spells a necessity to tackle it today, particularly in order to check for a better theory: is exilic literature a flash (or ashes) of a fashion or is it a tendency to reshape the map of writing?

This text will be dealing with two representative texts of exilic literature in the hope of contributing to a blueprint of such theory. My presumption is that two very different novels brought together by the common topic of exile should suffice to outline a territory that might call for a theoretical approach. Perhaps none of these novels might necessarily be judged as an event on its merits; however, the two of them could either make it to the level of an event or their analysis could demonstrate that they are but another exemplification of the already existing theoretical idiom.

The field is relatively new, which accounts for its conceptual diversity. 'Diasporic literature' seems to be an unlucky coinage as it reduces the literary function to a community of expatriates on an ethnic and/or religious basis. The concept fails to express the solitude and isolation or respectively the ways of integration or affiliation of those living abroad. Immigrant and respectively emigrant literature foreground the act of a human being rather than the features of his or her writing. To distinguish immigrant from emigrant literature makes sense only from the perspective of national literatures recognizing its emigrants writing abroad and its immigrants from abroad writing within the country. Trans-national literature remains confined to the logic and nomination of what it is about to overcome or transcend. From another perspective, trans-national appears to be attractive only as an anticipatory or futuristic concept, since even a global distribution is incapable of overcoming the spell of literary language and its publicity, including marketing, readership, awards and critiques. My preference for the concept of exilic literature is based on the assumption that it is literature that tackles the issue of exile and the latter motivates its artistic enquiries and enables us to present it as homeless, prodigal literature. In the course of the argument an alternative concept will be offered.

"Although the diversity of diasporic writing does not lend itself to abstract categorization, which would effectively erase or neutralize differences, the works discussed here share the common feature of being both creative and experimental and self-reflexive and theoretical", writes Azade Seyhan in her seminal book (2001, p.13). The texts to be discussed here will sail through the self-reflexivity test; they might be aptly described as both experimental and theoretical, and perhaps also "creative", whatever that means. Although they address exile in the traditional terms of loss, solitude, emptiness, nostalgia, etc., they refrain from making diagnoses or from indulging in somber self-lamentation. Exile is in focus, it is the alpha and the omega of those novels yet its interpretation goes well beyond the commonsensical articulations.

The novels of interest are *The Museum of Unconditional Surrender* by Dubravka Ugrešić and *Die Welt ist groß und Rettung lauert überall* (*The World is Big and Salvation Lurks around the Corner*) by Iliya Troyanov. The original reasons for this choice were both personal and national. A copy of Ugrešić's novel was signed to me in 2000 and I pledged to write something on this contemporary masterpiece. Ugrešić – one of the most renowned contemporary writers of exile – writes in Croatian and was born in Croatia, but her exile in the early 90s from Zagreb is prefigured by her Bulgarian mother's departure in the late 40s from Varna, my hometown. Troyanov's novel is loosely based on his personal experience of a 6-year-old boy whose parents took him along when they emigrated from Bulgaria. Troyanov writes in German yet he has spent many years outside Europe: ironically, his family emigrated, driven by the dream of the promise land of Germany, but a few months later his father was sent to work in Kenya, a fact that made of the future writer a professional nomad.

The two novels share enough to outline a vision on exilic literature. However, it is the disparity within the 'sameness' that would be of even greater interest. Each of the novels absorbs creatively the genres of memoir, autobiography and travelogue in favor of the omnivorous genre of the novel. Each of them insists on a non-linear evolution with abrupt leaps in time and place. Troyanov's novel is more scrupulous but also more fictional in dealing with time. Ugrešić is rather loose in specifying her timeframe once the exilic experience has been shared. The events unfold as the narrator returns home. Since she changes home for the suitcase (one of her metaphors for exile), the time-places start to blur, fuse and confuse, very much like the places in space: both are being traversed rather than visited or attended. Thus in both cases the story is told in an apparently disorderly manner. By contrast, Troyanov does stick to a plot, albeit suggested as a deliberately fake premise for the genuine happening. The plot involves a belated second life initiation, refiguring exile as an outlet for the wider world and thus overcoming the initial self-closure. In fact, this autistic isolation finds its counterpoint in Ugrešić's novel:

when her narrator refers to exile, her writing is permeated with
(quasi-) quotations from other people – friends, acquaintances,
strangers, writers, artists, etc., all of them sharing the destiny of exile.
Thus the parts dedicated to the actual experience of exile, be it in the
layered museum city of Berlin or during the innumerable journeys, all
these parts usher in an enormous amount of the speech of others: as if
the narrator has lost her ability to formulate any statement unless it is
endowed with someone else's authority or at least compassionate
presence; unless it is shared by – or ascribed to – someone else. This
creates an odd polylogue of solitary voices entangled in a talk at
cross-purposes. Although the dialogue seems to be doomed and the
statements remain wrapped in the quotation marks of their essential
detachment, the overall effect is less and more of a polyphony: rather,
these accumulated desolations create a Ligeti-like spatial, cosmic
vertigo.

Troyanov remains split between the requirements of exilic
literature and his adherence to the safe-side model of the modern
novel, whose narrative is based on a single story propped by two
characters, in this case those of an ailing exile and of his godfather
determined to rescue him. The novel sticks to a largely linear
narration: fleeing the country, followed by a spell in an immigration
camp and, after a 25-year leap into time, the central story of the main
characters' escaping the hospital, touring the world and returning
home to an anxious godmother unfolds. Still, the device of skipping
between unfinished, *in-medias-res* stories, with pauses, gaps and
omissions syncopates and energizes the writing. There is a telling
moment when the godfather urges his godson to put his fantasy at
work; we find him protesting a bit later: "Now you only enumerate,
Alex… You should use what you've seen, there should be a story, a
development!" (my translation from Bulgarian, p.89). In fact this wish
remains wishful thinking both for the godson and for the narrating
strategy of the novel in general. The reader will never be able to tell
whether the consistent failure of storytelling about the ailing émigré is
due to performative purposes or to inaptitude. The author remains
faithful to exilic literature's dictum to scatter a bundle of places and
moments whose interconnections, both temporal and causal, remain
loose. Thus while Ugrešić weaves her polyphonic texture out of
numerous voices, moments and places, all appearing in a motley,
ostensibly chaotic sequence, Troyanov starts with a rather elaborate

time alternation only to quietly abandon it, yielding before a much tidier narrative continuity. At the end of the day, however, both Troyanov and Ugrešić achieve the similar effect of the displaced and thus universal actuality of any moment by subjecting it to a seemingly whimsical order imposed by the power – or rather weakness – of memory.

Such trimmed and truncated narration is both typical and telling for the essence of exilic literature. The linear narrative unity projects a particular model of a world and a life incompatible with exile as both experience and inscription. Continuality, causality and completion are in fact implicitly discredited by exilic literature as the foundational myths and the ideal models of *oikos*-focused literature. Exilic experience or its faithful writing subverts the smooth linear narration even when the latter seems pursued by the author. Exilic literature avoids the fabulation principle that has held sway over the novel up to its postmodern condition. Exilic literature mixes outwardly random phrases – overheard or recalled – of casual people and texts. Thus its story-telling abstains from the triple unity of place, time and action as the even parts of Ugrešić's and Troyanov's entire text prove. The exilic narrative, as a rule, re-tells and quotes by heart, its stories failing to obtain beginning, climax or ending, their model being the one of the lame anecdote with a vague moral. The only things happening to the literary exile are the stories and the words of the other exiles – factual or actual, real or realized as such. The literary exile develops a certain sensitivity for those secondary, 'artificial' exiles who become such without abandoning their countries or being banned from them. The act of exile emerges as a peculiar event deprived of story but possessing the gift of identifying exile in all its reincarnations.

In effect, the shared poignant nostalgia for the past and the lost mother-country is balanced by (self) ironic disillusionment with regard to the spaces and times of refuge. By leaving home, the exile also forsakes the ideal and the idea of home: its abandoning reveals it as always already impossible or rather unfeasible. Thus the notorious shared love-hate for both the old and the new home-country is a somewhat misleading way to grasp the point here: that after the initiation of leaving there are no arrivals and returns left. The regular repertoire about exile such as the punishment of the past regarded as equal to a death sentence should be given perhaps a less sentimental interpretation: exile is a symbolic death with refused metempsychosis mainly because it subverts the idea of home and thus of return, of coming back, as well as of settling anew, of rebuilding a nest. Exile is but a symbolic act which makes space look like time – i.e. unidirectional and fluid.

Each of these novels is aware that home and home country are precious, not least because they have to do with the early years when things are not yet bound to be overlooked; they are here to stay in the mind due to the fresh cartridge of the memory machine. According to the two novels, exile is just an articulation, a sanction of a universal act: that of losing the early past of childhood and adolescence. Exilic literature is a literature of initiation not only as a sanctioned transfer into a new age and social status but also as a particular right to forget and neglect, to drop and omit, to leave behind, to be absent-minded in the literal awareness that the world is a place to be passed over. Therefore, an identity problem for exilic literature would be how to sneak away from the traditions of *Bildungs* and memoir literature, which deal predominantly with growing up: childhood, adolescence, youth... The figure of the left or lost home preventing return is a common allegory of the early years of unique experience when things happen for the first time. Abandoning home therefore might appear as an overdone attempt to displace the loss of the precious early years. Leaving home might be also a more ambitious attempt to prolong infinitely the slipping time of initial and unique experiences. In this sense the literature of loss obligingly becomes a literature of deferred loss of first-time things. The possibility of looking at it as an acted-out secondary childhood offers a tempting perspective on exilic literature. The immense heed that Ugrešić's and Troyanov's novel pay to the innocuous experience of infancy and youth there being represented as potentially prolonged through writing, sheds light on exilic literature as a loss of home and youth infinitely deferred through their artistic reproduction. Childhood, like living in poverty, in a poor country or age, informs experience with uniqueness, otherwise unattainable. However, such an exilic postponement is in fact incapable of overcoming the effect of secondary repetitiveness, of reiteration without authentic return. Thus the tempting hypothesis that exile is, apart from anything else, an ingenious attempt to prevent the real initiation of growing up or aging by providing an endless first-time experience appears to be ironically dismissed by exilic literature.

Exilic literature is about eternal non-arrival anywhere, and by the same token, about uniform failure and deferred return, very much evoking the short story by Thomas Bernhard, in which a train never exits a tunnel. It is a nomadic literature but not in the sense of beatnik road writing obsessed by the act and process of travelling. The gaze of the exile is struck by the peculiar myopia of a reflexive backward glance; when driving he/she finds his/her bearings through the rear-view mirror. This tendency has to do with the subverted cult for the first-time experience whose gift is actually or symbolically lost with the act of exilic initiation. As a result, the exile develops a kind of double vision: the fresh and juicy reappearance of the pre-exile experience, made up of first times, and the second, *post-mortem* life in exile, where things are deprived of depth and density but have absorbed instead the words and the dispersed stories of others. In effect, the world appears to be a dream-like surface reality stripped of its thickness and thus stultifying any scrutiny or devotion. The new places in such a world are not important in themselves but only to the extent that they trigger an associational chain shackling indiscriminately past and present. As if the actual world were structured like a language, i.e. like a dream. The place of photography in Ugrešić's novel is quite in point here: its 'semi-arrived' reality is haunted by reminiscent remnants deprived of depth, substance, density and thus of enigma. While reading Ugrešić's novel, one gets the impression that she knows and recognizes everything she encounters along her ramblings through Berlin. In the same vein, Bai Dan (the godfather) in Troyanov's novel manages to embroil his phlegmatic godson into a global trip; they are passing through cities as if without getting off from their tandem bicycle, as if going sightseeing in a dream. The small death of the exile makes everything beyond both unreal and all-too-well-known.

The paradox of childhood is the one of travelling: it always has to do with the memory of a happiness that should have been there and then but was neither then nor is it now, not least because its experience was missed then and is missing now. The happiness was there; it's just that there was no one to feel it. Now, when there is someone that can remember that past as happy, this happiness is past and its actual revitalizing is hampered by the very understanding that the moment is gone and has been missed; thus the moment now is filled with a sense of happiness as doubly lost – there and now.

Exile thus solidifies the paradox of childhood/travelling: visiting and memorizing a new place is possible to the extent that it triggers the experience of a previous place from the past, which in turn has evoked the vision of another place and time. Exile is a time machine providing justification for the most fundamental human experience of loss by giving it a (possible) name – exile. As a result, the pandemic sense of pain that pierces Ugrešić's novel and fails to work out in Troyanov's book, is always informed by the elegiac time and the intellectual distance of recognized, named and fortified loss. Hence, the restrained ironic slant, as if pain were perceived rather than suffered; a sense rather than a sensibility.

Exilic literature is thus made to a rare recipe, mixing reminiscence, myopia, boredom, irony and pain: a remembering wrapped in the painful experience of loss with untimely short-sightedness petrifying in the morbid boredom of the post-loss world.

The organizational principle of the novels is as efficient as it is reflectively laid bare. Ugrešić's novel is illustrated at the very beginning by the enlisting of what is found in the stomach of Roland the walrus. "The chapters and fragments which follow should be read in a similar way", continues the narrator and adds: "if the reader feels that there are no meaningful or firm connections between them, let him be patient: the connections will establish themselves of their own accord" (p.1). Troyanov's opening chapter also assembles fragments and episodes with no apparent cohesion or unity: the story of a family narrated with alternations from generation to generation borders on a perplexing exuberance that suggests family life's density and self-sufficiency. Still, Ugrešić is much more eager to report in advance the techniques that are to operate in her writing, not only as rhetorical or performative strategies but also as objects or activities that are to be discussed: a photography of unknown women, the family photo-album, the mother's bag, the museum of Odon von Horvath, organized around the principle of the writer's changing height, the writer's villa residency, sea-shore stone gathering, the magpie treasures of a madwoman… "I have no desire to be witty. I have no desire to construct a plot. I am going to … compile quotations" (p.11), says Ugrešić, quoting Shklovsky at the end of her first chapter, which brings to completion the arrangement of the bits and pieces she has brought to her exile, "all random and meaningless" (p.232).

Exilic literature's meaning is thus set to be hidden, promised and forever postponed. It is premised upon the paradigm of the random museum, of the photo-album, of the hobby-collection, of the autobiography. The reader might be tempted to subsume the exilic strategies under the postmodern trademark of encyclopedia but the proximity would be rather ostensible. The encyclopedic principle by definition excludes the decisive role of the selecting subject: encyclopedias are principally anonymous, unmarred by an author or authorship, as if impartial, non-subjective and in a sense inhuman. Memoir, autobiography, photo album, personal collection, even museum are made up of and for proper names of entities at hand. The goal of truth or reality *as such* yields before a subjective message behind the principle of arrangement. Yet the intentional message also happens to be subverted by the material itself, which resists, goes astray, dissociates, disperses, disengages. The exceptional presence of the visual arts in Ugrešić's novel perhaps has to do with the notorious mystery of curatorial practice, whose only warranted meaning and shared message is the curator's signature, the proper name standing behind. Exilic literature seems to owe more to curatorial art than to classical narration: the literary exile arranges the material at hand and in store like a curator, hoping for a split between the will to elicit its meaning and to let it grow and rise by its own will. The main attraction of such artwork comes from the challenging enigma of its organizational principle; a principle that not only allows but also stages breakages and failures of any conceivable logic, message, intention, meaning, sense, symmetry, regularity, proper beauty. To undo one's own game is as crucial for a good curator as it is for a literary exile.

Such (self-subversive) organizational principle raises a question: if exilic literature bets on the free assemblage of quotations, phrases, stories, bits and pieces, whose presumed unity is 'sanctioned' by the authority of a 'weak' author enlisting rather than narrating or 'figuring out', then how is this sort of literature different from the general postmodern strategy of collage/montage of genres, styles, times, borrowed characters, stories, even arts, books, discourses? Whereas the postmodern author pretends to be more or less dead by ordaining authority to language, literary tradition, history, geography, encyclopedia, archive, etc., the literary exile claims a restored authority by virtue of his/her trespassing and transgressing agency.

The literary exile gives up the agencies of totality – not only the one of God, but also the Aristotelian unities of narrative (action), of home (place) and of shared successiveness (time), let alone those of proper grammar, national literary language, genre, discourse, style, etc. The claim to being that unique unity, that vast vessel that witnesses an inimitable constellation of places, phases and stories is barely humble. By giving up the third person past tense panoramic viewpoint, exilic literature relinquishes the system of characters moving in their shared trajectories in time and space. The exile is principally incapable of possessing a companion, a satellite. The moment he or she acquires or allows one, he/she ceases to be an exile. Exile is a solitary human project whereas immigration implies dwelling, settling, taming the other(ness) back home, re-domesticating. The moment the adult ex-escapee in Troyanov's novel is involved in the 'tandem' tour with his godfather throughout the old and the new worlds, he becomes just another Ulysses on his way home, no matter how meandric his route might be. Genuine exilic literature actually challenges the basic literary structures of chrono-topos shared by two or more characters. The possible association with the picaresque novel, which is based on loosely connected episodes dominated by a protagonist, is also misleading because here the exile is outlined by his endemic inability to provoke a story. The exile is the one to whom nothing actually happens except for the words and the stories of others.[7]

The nomadic version of exilic literature thus overcomes exile by rendering it into a profession. Ugrešić's novel is an example of such travel turning into travels. Yet nomadic literature is by no means a travelogue. After discarding its narrative duties, nomadic literature seeks to get rid of another temptation – the one of the travel notes. Both Ugrešić and Troyanov solve this problem in a similar way: by fragmenting their observations, by cutting the pictures, by depriving the narrative of details, names and usage instructions, by revealing the 'insignificance', the dizzying inconspicuousness of cities, countries, peoples, life forms. This accounts for the fact that, contrary to the Aristotelian literary dictum, the character in exilic literature is far more important than action. The characters are somehow intact by what has been happening to them and preserve quite a paradoxical self-identity for creatures in a state of flux: as if after exile nothing can befall them. The unity is on the side of the character, not on the side of the story. Even more paradoxical is the fact that the unity of the character is achieved rather negatively, since the protagonist is more present through his or her absence. Both Troyanov and Ugrešić's narrators are much less present in their personal stories than in their way of telling the stories of others. The *I* seems to be possible only to the extent that it faces and transmits a world of selves with proper names.

Therefore it turns out that the postmodern/poststructuralist theory of writing based on difference is not immediately applicable to nomadic literature for a simple reason. A key postmodern narrating strategy translates the time axis into simultaneous space structures, transposes remote moments into neighboring places, which fuse with each other. Exilic literature is an anti-postmodern project as it resurrects the power and authority of the subject. The exiles – it turns out – are creatures who move permanently, cross borders, end up in different places but their travelling ethos makes them dwellers of a homeless time. This is another reason for the narrative to be systematically subverted. Nothing could actually happen when the logic of space-moving and place-changing depends on time flow rather than on any form of causality.

The present time in Ugrešić's mutant, archaeological Berlin consists of multilayered, molding impressions, words, thoughts, feelings of the others and the *I* indiscriminately. Hence the ineradicable sense of journalism, of report, of essay; and also of meditation, of interpretation. Another effect of this is the drive to trespass the borders between arts, discourses and mediums. Troyanov's character is almost dead in his present life but remains discursively rich, stylistically diverse and polyglot in general. Ugrešić's protagonist strolls through Berlin only to see it through and through as a palimpsest of her multilayered nomadic time rather than only as her dismantled Yugoslavia. Photography, visual art and urban guide-like writing are put together to resurrect what was, what has gone and what is to be by the power of memory as a model for exilic literature.

Such seemingly loose narrative structure in fact spots the main engine of the internal unity – the protagonist. Ugrešić's novel seems to have a more traditional first-person narrative structure, emulating the genres of a free-floating autobiography or a memoir. Troyanov's novel seems to play a more writerly game by shifting the narrating voices and thus developing a polyphonic effect. Yet it is the insipid taste of false expectations and annoyance with regard to *The World Is Big and Salvation Lurks around the Corner* that casts doubt on the entire field of emigrant literature, when it is incapable of achieving the status of nomadic writing. Although the author puts at work relatively modern or even contemporary narrative techniques – shifting of narrating voices, changing styles, alternating temporal layers and memory, vision and imagination respectively – his writing remains wearyingly overworked. The ultimate power of metonymy as a device for personal representation leads to an embarrassing reductive vision of what it is to be human. This is what does not work in Troyanov's novel and this is what relegates it to a decent example of emigrant writing: he thematizes what should not be talked about directly, i.e. feelings. His protagonist, on the verge of death because he has lost his zest for life, is saved by a character, combining a hero and a trickster. The protagonist's melancholy is rather phlegmatic, his lost ability to communicate blocks the access of the reader to his vague and dim tragedy. Thus when life should be regained and the character should appear cured, the tramp-like character of the story makes both the intellectual and the emotional contact shunt. An over-interpretation might go as far as to insist that such an effect is premeditated and the novel relies on such grotesque staleness in order to imply the effects of exile or immigration; however, boredom is barely an excuse.

Also, this appears rather too dated as a technique: the novel starts in a quasi-Joycean style borrowed from *A Portrait of the Artist as a Young Man* but changes its typical voice emulation of different ages for a Balkan ironically detached version of South American Magic Realism. Soon the latter is replaced by a technique of the late 19th century: a face-value set of expressions whose real meaning is given in brackets, for example: "oh, how sweet! (which is to say: positive predilection); what a caramel! (a sign of growing excitement), thou, empty sugar-bowl! (disappointment)…" (pp.26-27). It is as early as page 16 that the powerful title of the book is hazardously gambled away through the profane explanation that the sugar beet, languishing on local soil, has been safely replaced by the sugar-cane export from Cuba; the conclusion is that "big is the world and salvation lurks around the corner". Finally, the legendary-fairy-tale manner is also given up in favor of a leap somewhat 30 years later into the actuality marked by the unchallenged power of metonymy in dialogues like the following: "We are summoning aids for the military cemeteries", says the uniform. "I, instead, want to have my own Pershing", replies the pajamas" (p.32). The point is not only that this is not funny; not even that it is a dated way of writing - of course, one could imagine a kind of post-postmodern strategy of returning to the manners of the great realistic pre-war novel as a gesture of reaction and rejection. The point is that it is neither relevant nor efficient. This mix of Max Frisch with *roman nouveau* and a spoiled Aleko Konstantinov[8] leaves the impression of backward, obsolete writing. The narrative strategies are like trappings deprived of function: there are no gains neither in the sequential change of the narrators, nor in the change of styles. "Nobody cares a damn!" protests a Bulgarian character in English, leaving the impression of a broken polylogue.

Troyanov's writing feels concerned mainly with its sophisticated verbal command, cancelling any uncertainty. Troyanov seems to be tolerable through his well-earned techniques in the first part, alternating a semi-legendary semi-historically shaped pre-natal biography of the protagonist. Already the ending of this part, however, is consumed by the disturbing bulk of the novel. Troyanov is persuasive only when his narrator, a) has to rely on invention, fabulation and imagination, b) relies on the diegesis of epic narration and description, c) does not rely on memory, and d) his characters do not talk. In other words, Troyanov is unable to reproduce neither his own nor anybody else's experience and is even more helpless when his men and women have to converse. Thus Troyanov is least convincing in the exile components of his novel: the latter require knowing the languages of different people from different cultures and times. Troyanov is capable of emulating a realistic novel idiom from the first half of the 20th century but he is either predictable when he speaks from memory or artificial when has to mimic human conversation or speech. Troyanov leaves the impression that his (character's) exile has extricated him from any form of live experience and endowed him instead with the dubious gift of the books. Thus Troyanov's writing is again a regressive one; however, it does not look for refuge in his mother's tongue(s) but rather in the western tradition of the patriarchs of the novel. It is telling that his character is given the highly unlikely family name Luxov, i.e. Luxurious: such is the style, such is the legacy, but immigration never quite makes it to literary exile.

What saves this novel is its unpretentiously diligent and conscientious professionalism combined with a kind of disarmingly plain sincerity. Exilic literature has instead the task to correspond to its adjective and to overcome the notion of lost, forsaken or revoked national belonging, in order to have its say.

Ugrešić's play with the genres of testimony provides a much richer texture haunted by personal voices, stories and fates. Despite the radical perspectivism, her novel prefers to talk about the others. In fact, the only objects endowed with density in her writing are those with double refraction: the new nomad seems to be able to sense, feel, even love only through the senses, attitudes and bodies of the others. The latter accounts for the numerous thoughts and stories of people we are told little or nothing about. In fact, the narrator appears to be least persuasive when she takes the risk of playing confessional.[9] But Ugrešić's narrator is exceptionally convincing when she is hidden behind her characters and their stories. The reader communicates on a deeper level with the narrator when she seems to be most missing. The narrative's objective correlative of interpretive story-telling is decoded by the reader in an empathy which releases an ample amount of feelings, never mentioned or performed directly. Thus Ugrešić's narrator cautiously purifies and restricts her presence to the level of intellect and description, of irony and self-irony, of insight and its inevitable blindness whereas the reader accomplishes the work with empathy and compassion whose cathartic effect does not impair the intellectual aura while humanizing it.[10]

A somewhat paradoxical effect of the restored authority of the subject in her writing is the power of the knowing gaze. It sometimes robs the constructed world of its diversity and richness. The narrator's perspective is so powerful, so colorful, so devouring that the things and the characters appear deprived of autonomy, existence or enigma. The first impression is that the world told appears entirely interpreted, understood, disenchanted, and reduced to a particular meaning or message. This is often done in an extremely gifted and ravishing way: Dubravka Ugrešić seems to be aware of the predicament of the partial glance; therefore she elaborates her embroiled embroidery of unfolding irony, of insightful parody, of merciless truth-uttering. However, the effect is of a radical demystification that never doubts and whose answers always come out. Thus the powerful, convinced and persuasive voice of her overtly analytical narration leaves a somewhat discouraging impression of an all-too-trained and tainted vision, of a foretold and tamed voice. The narrator applies various techniques to avoid this disenchanted monologue of a life lesson known by heart: as already said, she multiplies the voices of alleged friends, acquaintances, occasional pick-ups, and overheard strangers; she periodically shifts the manner of narration (but never the style) by replacing description with someone's story, narration with moral or insight; she periodically flees from her own territory of words and thoughts to the neighboring ground of visual arts, photography, urban culture, new media, archaeology of everyday life and the art of sewing. She is almost ascetic in referring to the narrator's personal life. Deprived of the feather of personal destiny she resembles a new Wandering Jew or a Borges-like Shakespeare doomed to tell the stories of others. However, unlike the latter and very much like a cursed contemporary humanitarian, she knows and understands too much. Her writing on exile at times ferments to an overweening universal competence. Ugrešić's paresia at times appears to lead to a paralysis.

However, her exilic literature is also one of pain. This unique combination of competence, distance and irony and, on the other hand, of all-pervasive pain seems to require a better adjusted analytics, perhaps one that will reconsider the structure of Ugrešić's novel.

From the very beginning it declares a reluctance verging on abstinence regarding the narrative. Instead of narrating, it chooses to perform different genres, arts and practices in order to find proper instrumentaria fitting its main topic. The tools mostly consist of the working and the production of memory in a weird way of juxtaposing personal and historical bits and pieces. Those pieces are not meant to fit into a narrative structure while they are good at representing a biography.

Being a more or less reflected subversion of the narrative as literarily essential, exilic literature replaces its deliberate deficiency with adjusted borrowings (as I have already pointed out) from the poetics of different arts or practices. As a preliminary justification for their implementation, Ugrešić points to their artistic deficiencies which from a particular perspective might become aesthetic advantages, especially in the eyes of literary professionals. As if tucking under an aesthetic program, Ugreši ć comments on what she strives for along the very act of achieving it – the effect of the photo-album, of the museum collection, of the curatorial or artistic project, of autobiography. Traditionally the technique of stripping out the device generates estrangement or a *Verfremdungs* effect. A greater gain for Ugrešić would be, however, if such reflexivity did not prevent the text from achieving the effect of pain in the most elaborate manner of 'non-professional' imitation of professionalism.

From this perspective, it seems more plausible that exilic literature provides an alternative: in overcoming its own predicaments it turns into a literature we would call nomadic, which is the case with Ugrešić's novel, or to get domesticated as an incarnation of immigrant literature, which happens to Troyanov's book. Ugrešić's literary project is eager to suggest this essential immeasurability of *exile or whatever it's called*. The horizon of expectations with regard to the exiles is by no means one, unified or unanimous, yet it is not protected from being categorical: either cynically distrustful with regard to the pangs of banishment or superficially compassionate with regard to the doom of homelessness. Nomadic literature in fact strives to avoid the trap of *exile* as being automatically associated with *nostalgia* or *homesickness*. Perhaps a model for nomadic literature provides the allegory of the ex-colonies rather than the parable of the prodigal son. English allows this pun as mother country could both be 'mother land' and 'parent state'. Very much like the ex-colonies, which fought for and finally achieved their independence, the attitude towards the mother country is exceptionally ambiguous. From the perspective of the literary exile, the mother country is both a motherland and an ex-colonizer.

So what is the message behind these techniques of fragmentation, of piled bits and pieces of impressions, conversations, quotations, memories; what is the purport of this enigmatic museum of failed meanings at work here: mother's bag, photo album, odd collections, visual projects, flea market, concise biographies, all of them marked by descriptive excess and narrative deficit. The critical approach towards narrative as implicitly holistic and potentially totalizing should offer an alternative.

Undoubtedly, such an alternative model would claim to be more authentic, to render better the reality or its experience. Its alternative techniques are barely new, though. What is it that rescues nomadic literature from falling either into the modernist assemblage, or, from a different perspective, into the postmodern collage/montage? In other words, what makes the well-known organizational principle work and mean differently?

It does not take long for the reader, initially fascinated by the impression of aleatoricism, to figure out that Ugrešić's novel is in fact a hyper-organized text. It comprises seven parts, four of which – the odd numbers – appear under titles in German and stitch together numbered paragraphs, whose sequence is continued throughout the novel. As for the even parts, they are dedicated to different periods of the narrator's past, named after different individuals, who appear to be her anticipatory doubles: her mother in the second part; six encounters with exiles or internal émigrés in the fourth part (an overemotional American with a Polish name, an Indian, the Bulgarian grandmother, a lesbian couple, an East-German nostalgic cook, and a Portuguese one-nighter), the narrator's best female friends from the abandoned Croatia in the sixth part, who are six so as to correspond to the stories of the fourth part. It is also clear that the second and the sixth parts are organized around two photographs and that the photographic principle of writing is crucial for them. It is obvious as well that the first one and the seventh are mostly devoted to Berlin as a museum of incommensurability, whereas the third and the fifth focus on the exilic experience of the contemporary visual arts of assemblage. The mirroring principle of palindrome accomplishes the refined symmetries. Unsurprisingly, they are made to tilt, stumble and dismantle themselves at times: the story about the summer visits to the grandmother is placed not in the childhood part next to the extended portrayal of the mother but among the six travelogues; also, the description of Kabakov's art works is situated in the part devoted to the album as a family museum. Therefore, the reader faces an almost perfect yet delicately dynamized symmetry providing the beauty both of order and rhythm as well as of free associations and random choice.

Still, it remains unclear which of the strategies prevails: the one of disorderly and spontaneous assemblage or the one of symmetry, repetition, eternal return and all-encompassing self-identity and unity. Undoubtedly, Ugrešić's novel strives to achieve a subtle balance between order and disorder, between a meaninglessly bare life and its meaningful interpretation. The stakes are high because conveying life as it is and conveying meanings require strategies that are often at odds with each other. Such an elaborate organisation is the ultimate goal of any art above a certain level. Ugrešić's novel might be easily located among a lot of contemporary and older literary examples which equilibrate between order and disorder, between holistic sameness and scattered matchlessness. If the readers are unable to grasp this cautious balance, they might take the book as both disentangled and repetitive, chaotic and predictable, dispersed and self-reproductive, and thus possibly doubly far-fetched.

However, such a balance can hardly be peculiar to nomadic literature, whose theoretical particularity should not be restricted to its organizational principle of mirroring chaos or dismantling order. The readers might feel tempted to accept such elaborate disorder as charged to perform the very essence of exile, which, being deprived of the Aristotelian unity of time, place and action, i.e. of home-focused biography, replaces it with literary symmetries of radical displacement. It is therefore possible to see exile as triggering a whole system of transfers, displacements and sublimations, among which the one of interpreting exile as an essential human condition is the most salient.

However, if nomadic literature was about the painful experience of a home-freak, it would hardly be of particular interest. A reading that relegates exilic literature to the stage of homesickness, of suffering because of a particular loss and want, would miss the light side of the exilic moon. Ugrešić's writing provides ruses so as to enable a reading that creates hasty causal links between exile, nostalgia and pain. Yet the contradictions and the contrasting principles on which Ugrešić's novel stands subvert such causality.

First, the book is premised on the fundamental ambiguity of nostalgia as both homesickness and 'passed-time sickness'. The novel suggests that exile is both articulation and reworking of the initial initiation of growing up; certainly, with an element of counter-projection because leaving home to some extent displaces the growing up: the prodigal son – like a figural anticipation of the sci-fi astronaut moving at the velocity of light – is incapable of growing.

There is another misleading temptation, though: to treat Ugrešić's book as smart, ironic, and critical in the way and on the level her essays and interviews work. Nor should one be satisfied with interpreting Ugrešić's novel as a twofold critique with regard to both media and literature despite her sneering disdain concerning the narrative-dominated media. Ugrešić not only ironically reshuffles the postmodern idiom, but she is also entirely aware what she wants to achieve and where further to go. In fact, in the initial two chapters the narrator or the author herself formulates cautiously an aesthetic manifesto and an artistic program preparing the reader. The key points of this aesthetic program have to do with the powerful artistic weakness of both the photo-album and autobiography:

> Both the album and autobiography are by their very nature amateur activities, doomed from the outset to failure and second-rateness... There is only one thing that both genres can count on ... and that is the blind chance that they will hit upon the point of pain. When that happens ... then the ordinary amateur creation emerges victorious, on another non-aesthetic level, turning even the most splendid artistic work to dust. In literature such a work is an object of envy only for real writers. Namely, such a work has achieved with divine ease what they, for all their efforts, will never achieve. (p.31)

The narrator or the author dubs this pain a bit later the *invisible angel of nostalgia* that *brushes aside the daemons of irony*. Album and autobiography are the genuine genres of such amateur pain, which is endowed both with a universal, omnipresent status as well as with an ultimate subjectivity. This pain is also illustrated by the ambiguous genre of the primer, which is split between the naively blatant ideology of an imposed signified and the would-be radical innocence of an entirely empty signifier. In fact the pages that introduce the aesthetics of pain and authenticity are among the funniest, (self-) ironic and skillfully elaborate. With tongue in cheek they enlist the peculiar requirements for such an art of pain. It turns out it has to do with beauty and authenticity, with the beauty of truth, but also with the prosthesis of another language, be it the foreign language of English through which a girl shares the banal but intimate story of her just failed suicide (pp.34–35), be it the artificial language of the A grade essay whose contemplative-nostalgic tone "is transfixed by the precocious meditation on the leaves falling from the nearby tree and profound anxiety over the so-called transience of life" (p.33); be it the comparison between the literature of "stylistic tricks" and the one defined as "beautiful and authentic" (p.34).

Ugrešić is known for being a highly ironic as well as a pain-provoking author, her techniques recalling the authentic amateurism of the young couple who kiss like " 'amateurs' imitating ... the film stars". She names this "the pain of difference" and "the angel of nostalgia" and the sheer contradiction between the two expressions creates the field, where the contemplation over this kind of pain beyond aesthetics has to spread. Ugreš č's irony seems to target proper professional writers (of Iliya Troyanov's stripe) who pursue the effect of pain but who remain under the auspices of grand literature, genre and craft. But hers is also a self-irony, a warning that what she strives for is possibly a doomed effort because she is, after all, an all-too-professional writer whose pain is but a performed effect, a trick, a stunt.

Ugrešić's novel is bound not only to go beyond the media politics of exile as a phenomenon exhausted by perceptions like loss, separation, solitude and nostalgia, but also beyond her own poetics of the album, autobiography and other forms of (re)collection. What kind of pain is this? Where does it come from? What is it that feeds the sense of pain, displaced yet nagging? Ugrešić often writes about exilic experience, hers and others'. However, in passages endowed with exceptional clarity and profound reflexivity she refrains from the notion of exile as an epitome of nostalgia, loss and privation and reconsiders it as an option, opportunity and optics. Her literature in fact elicits a pain, alternative to the one of nostalgia. Not only the all-pervasive irony but also the gains of the exile's hazardous game are to be reckoned here. Exilic literature is capable of overcoming exile as a predicament evolving into a nomadic attitude.

A prerequisite for such an attitude is a demystification of the notion of home, a debasement of the economy of *oikos*. Exile draws upon the figure of nostalgia: craving to return home where home works as a figural extension of receptacle and thus enables a pre-symbolic pure communication and provides place and function. Thus *oikos* makes sense as a figure of incontestable order; it simultaneously delimits and discerns objects through their applications and humans through their roles, thus involving them in a productive communication. The figure of home appears authoritative even for Heidegger, as his notorious phrase about language as a home of being proves. So a subversion of *oikos* undertaken by exilic literature echoes overtones of a philosophical challenge. *The Museum of Unconditional Surrender* gets its genuine power from the alternative experience of defying the economy of *oikos*.

Such defiance is never a direct attack. It is refracted through the structure of the novel, which relies on a particular organizational principle. This principle emerges in its purer form in the uneven shorter parts dedicated to the experience of Berlin as a city of emigrants and exiles, national museums and international artists, historical layers and flea markets. Those relatively equal and short pieces of writing alternate between personal observations, personal art projects and exchanges with people who never make it to the status of characters. All those brief pieces of writing in fact are never accomplished but rather halted, interrupted, cut off. In fact, with time they develop a certain wholeness and completeness, implanted in the pieces of writing through their recursive openness and inconclusiveness. This effect of indifference between totality and fragmentation elicits a peculiar reader response of *panting*, a word that tellingly comes from the Greek *phantasioun,* 'cause to imagine'. This panting, which stems from the self-exhaustion of any part in itself and from the alternative drive to continue because of a peculiar insatiability, produces the unique rhythm of Ugrešić's writing. The effect is that this rhythm conveys the special nomadic experience beyond exile and its grievances. In exilic writing it also produces the pulsation of indifference between persistence and distraction, between adherence and non-commitment, between completeness and inconclusiveness, and at last between indifference and love; a pulsation intentionally unable to provide a home to any meaning or message.

There is a tender curiosity, a distracted persistence and an oblivious reiteration in the way the narrator examines the post-exilic world. Hers is not just the sharp eye of a constant stranger trained to find its bearings in any environment. The descriptions given and the stories told project a gaze that is unable or unwilling to provide home to what is seen and described. Through Ugrešić's eye and writing, things remain somehow detached, displaced and dispatched, uprooted and orphaned, separated from their origin and history, and thus stripped of self-identity and inner integrity. Ugrešić's novel describes her exilic places in the estranging and defamiliarising way that implies and imposes their homelessness. Surprisingly the same turns out to be valid for the stories referring home. The detached, displaced homelessness of the places and the things narrated appears therefore to be the inherent style of Ugrešić's writing. It crystallizes in a poetics shirking the economy of oikos. Exile provides both an optics and a perspective for shaking up the natural essentiality of home and home country. Exile is as much an experience of loss as it is a response to a certain ennui of *home*, a response to home's parochialism, provincialism, congestion with national and family 'values and truths' etc. Exile reveals home and its values as largely ideological and historical constructs. From the homesick perspective of exile home suddenly emerges as a sick home. Departure turns any return into arrival elsewhere. Leaving home thus remains forever marked by the sense of irretrievable loss but also by the perspective and prospect of turning the world outside into a 'home'-proxy. The exile becomes an *oikos*-promiscuous creature discovering the relative *proxy-mity* of home as such. Leaving home is replaced by an entering language as always already other and only as such a possible home for being.

What the exile discovers is the home as sick and the world outside and abroad as a dwelling space, or rather, time. True, the world can become home only as far as the very concept of home is reconsidered from the perspective of a resurrected and revitalized nomadic ethos of temporariness, interchangeability and multiplicity, i.e. the ethos of indifference. Such attribution of a new meaning to the concept of home does not pass without pain, though.

So let us go back to the pain induced by Ugrešić's writing. This pain feels like a sweet pain. Yet it is neither voluptuous nor lustful. Being intensively sweet, this pain is on the verge of leaving a heart *high-sorrowful and cloy'd*, to borrow from Keats. It makes it poignantly sweet, a bitter-sweet pain. Actually, I feel that (my) English falls short of describing this pain as the *nostrum* that Ugrešić's novel offers Such a peculiar combination of tenderness and sadness has a special place in Christian Orthodoxy. Expressed with the word 'умиление' in different Slavic languages, it might be translated – poorly – with 'endearment'. *Умиление* actually sounds close to both 'humility' and 'humiliation', both of which come through Old French from Latin *humilis* 'low, lowly,' from *humus* 'ground.' *Умиление* or the Greek notion Ελεούσα – 'caressing' – is among the key visual hypostases of Our Lady and has to do with *милост,* i.e. 'mercy', and έλεος – compassion, sympathy, empathy. In Orthodox iconography this particular hypostasis depicts Virgin Mary and the infant Jesus cheek to cheek, which symbolizes the annihilation of the distance between the human and the divine through the power of love. This proximity is also full of anticipation and preliminary knowledge about the inevitable separation that sacrifice involves, and more generally, it all applies to a sense of loss and death. In Greek art Ελεούσα has also been called Γλυκυφιλουσα, 'sweet loving' or 'sweet kissing'. The key to grasping the pain, which Ugrešić's exilic writing induces, lies in the element of compassion and of endearment to the point of mutual melting down; besides, this pain involves the awareness of inevitable separation and mutual loss; there is also the element of humility about one's own human origin and limitations. Ugrešić's endearing pain is full of *умиление* and humility, the latter grasped in its intimate, original relation to the soil, the fertile black earth of *humus*, of *чернозем*. In a word, what Ugrešić's prose arouses as a reaction – emotional but also cognitive – is a peculiar pain that is also the *nostrum* she is offering to her readers.

It is perhaps but a coincidence that *nostrum*, coming from the Latin word for 'our', and *nostos* 'returning home' sound close enough to build a connection between *nostalgia* and *nostrum*; as if the pain (*algia*) for home might be treated only through the unreliable *nostrum* of endearment to and love for the world after and beyond home (*oikos*). Nostalgia and the pain of difference, which Ugrešić tries to reconcile, could be put together if only the pain for both *nostos* and *nostrum*, for returning home and returning back to one's own past, finds its nostrum in the in-difference within a world taken as Home. Ugrešić's pain is one that goes together with *умиление*, endearment towards a world outside and abroad, where the concepts of exile and home become paradoxically and productively in-different. If nostalgia, this Swiss illness, homesickness, Heimweh, is a psychoanalytically regressive reaction, Ugrešić's pain in fact feeds on this nostalgia, be it a pain for home or for the past. But by thriving on it, it coins a substantially different pain, which is capable of incorporating both the daemon of irony and the angel of nostalgia.

Even before promoting her aesthetic manifesto Ugrešić paves the way for the already discussed crucial feature of her writing: her stubborn refraining from narrativity. It is known that since Aristotle the narrative, plot or mythos requires a conflict as the basis of action. In Ugrešić's novel, however, there is neither action, nor conflict *per se*. There are many characters there but none of them is in fact involved in any kind of action or conflict with the I-narrator. Even when Doty's story is told, the sneering irony and sweeping abjection come from aside and from an estranging distance, as if the characters were already separated by borders and other boundaries. In fact, not only conflict and action are missing from this novel – there is one more fundamental absence. It would be difficult to find today such a relatively long novel that can manage without the help of love. The two love moments are rather about its absence, if not impossibility. Yet the pain that is Ugrešić's nostrum reminds a phenomenon known as love pain or pangs of love. But how could one experience love pain when in the whole novel love, the conflict and the action of love, the happening between two persons are the most salient missing piece?

What seems to be missing in this novel and in nomadic literature in general is love as an interpersonal act, actuality and action, because it has been replaced by an omnipresent love without defined or stable objects. This new nomadic love is endearingly painful because the objects are inevitably abject, doomed to be abandoned insofar as they are visited. This nomadic love of endearment and pain actually dissolves the getting together and the separation within a post-exilic world. Love in exilic literature seems impossible and missing because this literature is all about love; a new love for a world that could never again be appropriated and possessed. Exile appears to be this love without possession, without ownership. This is not so much unwillingness to possess and to be possessed; it is rather the realized incapability, the emerging impossibility to have if one is to **become** in time rather than to **be** in space. This is a love beyond coveting and longing, beyond desire and will. Instead, this is a love for the one, which is neither the other nor the same, and thus defies both the logic of identity and the logic of difference by presenting them as indifferent. Such an endearing love pain of *умиление* offers its own logic of indifference *per se,* i.e. the exiles' apparent un-concern or nonchalance, their ostensible inability to become attached or to home in on their new places, is based on the general impossibility and on their personal inability to tell anymore the difference between home and exile, and by the same token, between Self and Other. Ugrešić's indifferent love for the world as a temporary abode treats the notions of home and exile with indifference and as in-different. Such an indifferent love for places and human beings grants genuine power to Ugrešić's writing. It presents it as an ultimate incarnation of a literature that overcomes its cornerstone – exile itself – in a nomadic vision of indifference that loses both the sameness and the difference but gains the power of non-possession, of homelessness as a way towards dis-otherness. The logic of indifference is the one of non-belonging but also of the situational sheltering without cathexis.

Now we feel much closer to the message of the perception set up and induced by Ugrešić's nomadic literature. Its pain is not to be reduced to an emotive response; its sensual aspect develops its cognitive counterpoint. The sweet pain of endearment towards a post-home world crystallizes in the indifferent love which subverts simultaneously the identity-possessive self and the otherness-obsessive difference. Such an indifferent love overcomes those two poisonous love drives of possession of the other and of giving oneself over to the other. Indifferent love is a prerogative of the new nomad who (dis)misses the difference between home and abroad in the entirety of their meanings. It is exactly this indifferent love without returns and arrivals, without identity and otherness that makes possible the interactive co-operation between nostalgia and *the pain of difference*. It is this indifference that slips from both sameness and difference, which at the end of the day transforms exile into a nomadism which closes the power cycle of *oikos* as an instance of dividing us from them, ours from theirs, one's own from someone else's, family from strangers, here from there, home from abroad, the same from the other. Therefore the nomadic indifferent love is the only love that is not based on the imperialism of choice and segregation, of favouring and discrimination, of dialogue and exchange.

Thus exile is not about exile in itself. Exile becomes an entity only to the extent that it opens up for a nomadic attitude based on indifferent, indiscriminate love for a world structured as a journey rather than as a home, as time rather than as place. Although it certainly builds on the existentialist and Christian tradition of abandoning home, the nomadic upgrade goes beyond exile as a human condition. For many, exile remains in the grips of the usual suspects: loss, solitude, nostalgia, etc. But to the extent that it is fixed or displaced by the indifferent love for a world marked as an anticipated loss, it advances a new nomadic lifestyle and another set of values. The complex of *умиление* or *Ελεούσα* projects human and God as almost fused, without a distance in between. Yet this fusion remains a self-subversive figure as it reveals itself as a rhetoricized wishful thinking. The propinquity and intimacy in fact discredit the fusion as always already lost. What is left after the initial separation and loss is a striving and a pursuit of an unattainable fusion, be it the one between man and God, man and the world, the self and the other. If home is a replacement for the initial loss of the receptacle, then exile is the initiation of the second birth. Thus the indifferent nomadic love for the world as the next stage of womb/home comes to fix both the initial loss and the secondary initiation of exile. Yet this love remains transfixed with the pain of умиление/Ελεούσα/endearment because of the realized impossibility of fusion with a world, which is entirely homeless and womb-less. Even endowed with the nomadic love which provides in-difference between the self and the world, the new nomad remains in the grips of his or her ironic pain because the world itself defies its perception as a home or as a womb. Thus nomadic love is an ironic sublimation of exile as another death rehearsal. Indifferent love is an individual proxy-revolution after the discredited revolutions of the masses. It does provide an ironic yet loving exit from the historically constructed and already obsolete culture of *oikos*.

Yet what is wrong with home? Where does the crisis of the *oikos* institution come from?

The interpersonal situation, whose home is home itself inverts the meanings of the verbs, overturns the words by imposing the language of imperatives. It presupposes an interpersonal situation under the auspices of the imperative mood, in which everybody talks to the others in orders while his or her actions are expressed by the requirements or requests of the others. Home, *oikos*, is the inherent space of the imperative as the cornerstone of communication among one's own people: be it the simple case of the wanting child, be it the perfidious asking or begging of the parents, siblings, spouses, friends... The economy of *oikos* is based on imperatives, on 'give!' in particular, which implies in fact the action of taking.

Abandoning home literally or rather metaphorically is the first step of breaking the spell of the imperatives' spurious naturalness. The initial replacement of the imperatives with questions, with interrogative sentences marks the first figural act of exile. Exile as a precondition for the nomadic indifferent love for the world cannot break the economy of taking and giving but is still able to replace the *oikos* economy of imperative imperialism with the alternative economy of asking, of formulating questions. In Ugrešić's novel it is indicative that the four parts on exile are named in German – a language announced as unknown – with two of the parts formulated like questions: *Was is Kunst?* and *Wo bin ich?* The experience of exile appears to be all about asking and questioning, often without answers and without expectations, not least because imperatives appear to be obsolete or impossible, which means that the questions cannot be (mis)taken for imperatives. The nomadic condition of love questions things, places and people as indifferent from/for me and thus free from interest, free from the power of imperatives. Nomadic exile reveals home as a disenchanted imperative and the globe as an entity to inquire about.

Thus the nomadic indifferent love brings back the enchantment with a world disenchanted by the spell of imperatives. Being traditionally associated with the poignant experience of preliminary death and death rehearsal, being marked by the regressive stain of driving back home, to one's mother and motherland, exile in its artistic re-appropriation becomes a time machine. It helps overcome nostalgia as an epitome of death in favor of a new eventful love – the brand of nomadic indifferent love in the form of a permanent query, which means regaining human immortality in the womb/home of the globe. Nomadic literature is about the power of indifferent love to move as a time machine through the time layers in the global nomadic space. By subverting the power of imperatives indifferent love in fact dismisses the power of causality usurped to the utmost by the instance of questioning the instant. Indifferent love wraps in painful and ironic умиление the world. By loving indifferently the writing nomad unwraps the Globe in countless question marks. The Globe thus appears as the homeless womb. With its sweet painful panting of birthgiving.[11]

Notes

[1] There is no shortage of ideological motivations in the recent interest in diasporic literature: the fresh blood donated by the ex-colonies has galvanized the cultural corpus of the mother countries, etc. On the other hand, exilic literatures in Eastern Europe have partly filled the gap after the discredited socialist literature. When it turned out that locker literature either does not exist (as in Bulgaria) or is unable to replace the would-be 'fake and phoney' literature of the communist past, the literary curricula ushered in 'emigrant literature'. Nevertheless, the historical and cultural dynamics that brought to the fore exilic literature deserves – and receives – substantial attention. Exilic literature is perhaps the only genuine phenomenon of the last decades in the wake of sex, gender, sexual orientation, race, class, etc. Thus, very much like its predecessors, exilic literature faces the paradox of choice: whether it prefers to be

admitted to the established canon through its enlargement, or it would put up with the establishment of alternative canons, whose differentiation would be forever threatened by some level of ghettoization.

[2] For years Bulgarian critics at home, including myself, have abstained from treating as Bulgarian a literature written abroad by immigrants in foreign languages, since those writers opted for a new cultural affiliation, i. e. they do not belong to the national culture. However, it turned out that none of three internationally acclaimed Bulgarian writers – Kapka Kasabova, Dimitre Dinev and Iliya Troyanov – minds a victorious return to and recognition in their forsaken homeland. They have given up their initial abstention and have eagerly re-emerged to become instances in the national culture.

Yet it was hardly their own idea: two alternative projects to save literature compete today in Bulgaria. The first one relies on translating, promoting and selling abroad the recent outstanding Bulgarian production. So far, however, its international face has been outlined by a bunch of poets and writers who mostly owe their translations to personal connections with translators and publishers. A rampant example is the married couple Mirela Ivanova – Vladimir Zarev, who have achieved unsuitably representative status as Bulgarian writers in the German-speaking world.

The other strategy bets on 'Bulgarians' living abroad and writing in major languages, particularly if they occasionally accept and proclaim their Bulgarian descent, which usually happens when an award arises on the horizon. Writers like Tzveta Sofronieva, Milena Fučedžieva, Vladislav Todorov, Lubormir Kanov, Roumiana Zaharieva, Dimitar Inkiov, Assen Assenov, Zlatko Enev, Antoaneta Slavova, Nikolaj Atanassov have been working and writing abroad long enough to be almost forgotten. The recent upsurge of mutual interest apparently has to do with the proven literary success of the mentioned above ex-Bulgarians. Kapka Kassabova, Dimitre Dinev and Iliya Troyanov, known respectively in the East Pacific English and in the German worlds, have just been recognized as a chance for Bulgarian literature to overcome its anonymity. Bulgarian literature in general and its contemporary version in particular are perhaps the least known in the whole of Eastern Europe. After – unsuccessfully – we tried to attribute Bulgarianness to intellectuals like Tzvetan Todorov, or Julia Kristeva, or John Atanassov, the time has come for 'our' writers abroad to be summoned back.

[3] As a minor literature on loss and violated rights exilic literature is a commissioned art. Although it is known that literature's mimetic bond is massively overrated, the experience of exile provides a fertile soil for a typical literary cultivation. There is a hidden aesthetic ideology in the alleged or promoted correspondence between the human condition of exile and its counter-establishment articulation. On the market of democracy its critics and its outcasts are the most suitable dummies proving its potential for self-improvement. By translating marginal or subversive authors, and by envisaging this act as an agency for establishing a new European identity, the cultural and academic institutions in fact enter into – blindly or not – a structural collaboration with political power.

[4] The debate being elaborated at length in authoritative Azade, Seyhan, 2001.

[5] The hope that the trial of rupture, dispersion, fragmentation and "neither here, nor there" (non-)belonging would safely lead to another continuity, thus negotiating the new cultural identities of contemporary Europe, implies that the critical, subversive

and thus heuristically productive potential of a postfeminist/postcolonial theory is meant to be sacrificed in the name of constituting a new Europeanness. It is both tempting and soothing to imagine such Europeanness as a lapidary version of the dispersed non-identity of immigrants and exiles, of diasporic and trans-national writers and artists. Yet it would be another theoretically forged utopia, straggling behind the arts, sciences, and businesses of a globalizing world. The perfume of sacrificial heroization of exilic literature may thus turn flat.

[6] An element, act or figure of exile is, or should be, a general property or a prerequisite for any artistic creativity. Kristeva and others have suggested that going into language can be interpreted as a final act of banishment from the pre-linguistic spaces and practices of genuine communication, whose perfect and perhaps idealized model is the one within the mother's womb. Therefore, exile is a general human condition. Literature as the only discourse that simultaneously recognizes, performs and subverts the fundamental exile of human existence, and whose country of exile is again language itself, is a theoretical utopia which has not exhausted yet its heuristic potential. (See Kristeva, 1984; '82; '86; '91).

[7] Perhaps this explains why exilic literature is particularly good at giving titles, at naming and nominating: it remains on the side of linguistic (un)translatability rather than on the side of mythos, i.e. of narrative universality. By crossing the border of the home country, the literary émigré strides from the world of things into the world of their multiple partial translations. This, according to Walter Benjamin in "The Task of the Translator" in *Illuminations*, New York: Schocken Books, 1968), is the only way to unveil the genuine pre-language before Babel through accumulation.

[8] A paradigmatic Bulgarian writer of (1863–1897), known for his travelogue *Do Čikago i nazad* (To Chicago and Back, 1894) and his masterpiece *Bay Ganyo* (1896), an annecdotal narration about a Bulgarian touring Europe.

[9] The Lisbon love affair is the most dubious among the *Six stories with the discreet motif of a departing angel*; it looks like a patch, like a foreign body in the novel's centre. It is either a random lapse into a more personal tone or just a cunning strategy, as the unexpected journalism with political overtones in the opening of the part suggests.

[10] The dialogue of the reader simultaneously with the narrator and with her characters is a trade mark of exilic literature. Because of the ubiquitous pain, the narrator seems to be exiled also from the country of situational feelings and unmediated emotions. The craft of writing on exile requires the narrator to play the role of pure mediator between a reader and an experience.

[11] The text may well arouse suspicions that the suggested approach towards exilic and respectively immigrant and nomadic literature is based extensively and exceptionally on Ugrešić's novel *The Museum of Unconditional Surrender*, and therefore remains an outsider with regard to the contemporary debate on issues like exile, nostalgia, contemporary nomadism, etc. For example, it is clear that my disqualifying, or rather, *looking-for-alternative* attitude towards nostalgia should delineate its standing in terms of Svetlana Boym's recent classic (Boym 2001). Boym's perception of nostalgia as a historical and modern disease seems to be logical and understandable as she treats nostalgia as another incarnation of counter-modern – or off-modern in her language – compensatory response to the deficiencies and exigencies of modernity. She also insists that nostalgia is still generally an incurable disease no matter how metaphorical the perspective.

My point, on the contrary, is that the nomadic response of indifferent love emerges as a medicine, or at least as a *nostrum* for the pain or for the drive of *nostos*. The nomadic attitude as it has been described is the main achievement I elicited from Ugrešić's writing. In her case, the nomadic response reaches the plane of a particular purity and density, which accounts for my devotion to her version of nomadic love.

In a recent publication, Svetlana Boym makes the following observation: "If in the 1980s artists dreamed of becoming their own curators and borrowed from the theorists, now the theorists dream of becoming artists. Disappointed with their own disciplinary specialization, they immigrate into each other's territory. The lateral move again. Neither backwards nor forwards, but sideways. Amateur's out takes are no longer excluded but placed side-by-side with the non-out takes. I don't know what to call them anymore, for there is little agreement these days on what these non-out takes are.

But the amateur's errands continue. An amateur, as Barthes understood it, is the one who constantly unlearns and loves, not possessively, but tenderly, inconstantly, desperately. Grateful for every transient epiphany, an amateur is not greedy." ("Nostalgic Technology: Notes for an Off-modern Manifesto" – http://www.svetlanaboym.com/manifesto.htm).

Well, Barthes' and Ugrešić's amateur seems to be in-different from our nomad full of painful endearment towards a globe deprived of drive for womb and home.

Bibliography

Ugrešić, Dubravka. 1999. *The Museum of Unconditional Surrender*. London: Phoenix. (*Musej bezuvjetnee predaje*. 1996. Beograd: Samizdat B92; Zagreb: Konzor, 2001–2002)

Troyanov, Iliya. 1996. *Die Welt ist groß und Rettung lauert überall* (*The World is Big and Salvation Lurks around the Corner*). Munich: Carl Hanser.

Hančev, Veselin. 1966. 'Romansero za Hose Sanča' in: *Stihotvorenija* (Poems) Sofia: Bălgarski pisatel.

Benjamin, Walter. 1968. 'The Task of the Translator' in: *Illuminations*. New York: Schocken Books.

Boym, Svetlana, 2001. *The Future of Nostalgia*. New York: Basic Books.

Deleuze, Gilles and Félix Guattari. 1986. *Kafka: Toward a Minor Literature* (tr. Dona Polan). Minneapolis: University of Minnnesota Press.

Kristeva, Julia. 1984. *Revolution in Poetic Language*. New York: Columbia University Press.

— 1982. *Powers of Horror: An Essay on Abjection*. New York: Columbia University Press.

— 1986. 'Stabat Mater' in *The Kristeva Reader* (ed. Toril Moi). Oxford: Basil Blackwell.

— 1991. *Strangers to Ourselves* (tr. Leon S. Roudiez). New York: Columbia University Press.

Seyhan, Azade. 2001. *Writing outside the Nation*. Princeton, NJ: Princeton University Press.

Contributors

Elka Agoston–Nikolova, PhD in Slavic literature. Lecturer of South Slavic Languages, Balkan Studies (folklore and ethnic identity); Studies on Central and South Eastern Europe (history and culture); and Gender issues (representations of women in literary texts – modern Bulgarian literature).

Publications on issues of oral literature, gender studies, ethnic and national identity. Most recent participation in History of the Literary Cultures of East-Central Europe – (vol. 4 forthcoming: *The Epic Heroes of the Balkan Slavs*), John Benjamin Publishing Co.

Penka Angelova, professor of German and Austrian Literature at the University of Veliko Tǎrnovo (Bulgaria) and German language literature and European civilization at the University of Russe (Bulgaria). She is also Chairwoman of the International Association *Elias Canetti*.

More than 100 publications in international volumes and journals Germany, Austria, Hungary, Poland etc. Awarded Austrian honorary award in science and art (2002) and the literary prize of the city of Russe (2006).

Recent publications: *Ich sehe was, was du nicht siehst*, Röhrig Verlag. 2002; and *Elias Canetti. Spuren zum mythischen Denken*, Zsolnay Verlag. 2005.

Nikolaj Aretov, Ph.D and Dr. Hab. Disertation. Lecturer (University of Sofia and the New Bulgarian University). President of the Bulgarian Society for 18th century studies, senior editor in Kralica MAB publishing house, editor of the journal *Literaturna Misǎl*.

Among his major publications are: *Dimitǎr and Rahil Dushanovi*, 1988; *The translated prose from the first half of the 19th century*, 1990; *Bulgarian Renaissance and Europe* (1995, 2nd ed. 2001); *Vasil Popović. His life and his work.*, 2000; *National Mythology and National Literature*, 2006.

Ellen Elias–Bursać, translator of novels and non–fiction by Bosnian, Croatian and Serbian writers (David Albahari, Svetlana Broz, Slavenka Drakulić, Slobodan Selenić, Antun Š oljan, Dubravka Ugrešić). Her translation of David Albahari's novel *Gotz and Meyer* was awarded the National Translation Award by the American Literary Translators Association in 2006. She has co-authored an award winning textbook for the study of Bosnian, Croatian, Serbian with Ronelle Alexander, now in its 2nd edition, and has written a study on the poet Tin Ujević and his work as a literary translator.

Maja Bojadžievska, professor of General and comparative literature (SS. Cyril and Methodius University, Skopje). In 1998 she received her Ph.D. degree in Comparative Literature with her thesis on the myths of sexuality in the modern novel.
Some of her major publications include: *Writing in Neutrum (cynical essays)*, Skopje, 2007; *The Novel: Status, Interpretations and Perspectives*, Skopje, 2004; *Imaginary Women: coming out of the shadow,* 2001.
(Published translations of Gilbert Durand, Jacques Derrida, Gilles Deleuze, Julia Kristeva, Miglena Nikolchina, A.R. Radcliffe-Brown, Jean-Pierre Vernant, Dubravka Ugrešić).

Raymond Detrez, professor of Slavic Studies and Balkan History at the Universities of Gent and Leuven. Has published numerous books and articles on Balkan history, minority policy and nationalism in Southeastern Europe. Some of his major works are: *De sloop van Joegoslavie. Het relaas van een boedelscheiding,* 1996; *Kosovo. De uitgestelde oorlog,* 1998; *Historical Dictionary of the Republic of Bulgaria,* 1997.

Dimitar Kambourov teaches literary theory at Sofia University. He is a co-director of the "Literary Studies" MA Programme in Slavic Studies at Sofia University. Publishes on literature, arts, culture, politics, gender, the Balkans, etc. Dimitar Kambourov is the author of *Yavori i Kloni* (Sycamores and Branches, 2003), *Bălgarska Poetičeska Classika* (Bulgarian Poetic Classic), co-editor with Irina Novikova of *Men in the Global World: Integrating Post-Socialist Perspectives*, Helsinki, 2003, and *Pro Art/Арт Про*. Maria Vassileva and Dimitar Kambourov (eds). Sofia, 2007.

Goce Smilevski (1975, Macedonia) has a MA in Gender Studies (Central European Unjiversity, Budapest) and MPhil in Comparative Literatures (SS. Kiril I Metogij University, Skopje). His novel

Conversations with Spinoza (2006) has been translated into several languages, including English.

Tzveta Sofronieva was born in Sofia, Bulgaria in 1963 and, after residences in Canada, U.S. and Great Britain, lives now in Berlin. She studied Physics, holds a doctorate in Cultural Studies and attended a Poetry Master Class of Joseph Brodsky. She edited the collections "Forbidden Words" (2005) and the "Web Streaming Poetry" (2010) and is the founder of the intercultural networks of the same name. Her recent volume with poetry in German, *Eine Hand voll Wasser* (2008), is currently being translated into English with a grant from PEN American Center's translation fund. Tzveta Sofronieva was awarded Germany's *Adelbert-von-Chamisso-Förderpreis* in 2009 and has recently been appointed writer-in-residence at the Max Planck Institute for the History of Science in Berlin. For more information visit www.tzveta-sofronieva.de.

Goran Stefanovski, writer, dramatist, scriptwriter. Born in Macedonia, worked in Yugoslavia as one of its most prominent theatre professionals until the early 1990s. Now based in Canterbury, UK. A reputation of uncompromising treatment of the themes of identity, cultural history and politics. Among his major works: *Hotel Europe*, 2000; *Sarajevo*, 1995; *Tales from the Wild East*, 2005; *The Demon of Debar Maalo*, 2006; research into the Methodology and Theory of Scriptwriting – *A Little Book of Traps*, 2002. In 2007 he won the International Literary Prize Vilenica.

Dubravka Ugrešić, born in former Yugoslavia, degrees in Comparative Literature and Russian Language at the University of Zagreb and worked for twenty years at the Institute of Literature (Zagreb), as a writer and literary scholar. She left Croatia in 1993 and is currently living in Amsterdam. Among her major works are: *The Culture of Lies*, 1998; *The Museum of Unconditional Surrender*, 1998; *Thank you for not Reading*, 2003; *Lend me your Character*, 2004; *The Ministry of Pain*, 2005; *Nobody's Home*, 2007, *Baba Yaga Laid an Egg*, 2009.

She has been awarded numerous literary awards: the Heinrich Main Prize (2000), the Austrian State Prize for European Literature

(1999), Versetsprijs 1997, Kunstenaarsverzet; Premio Feronia (2004).,
PEN Writers in Translation Award, UK (2006).

Chantal Wright is assistant professor in the Department of Foreign
Languages and Literature at the University of Wisconsin-Milwaukee.
She is the recipient of an award from PEN American Center's 2009
Translation Fund in support of her translation of Tzveta Sofronieva's
Eine Hand voll Wasser.

www.ingramcontent.com/pod-product-compliance
Lightning Source LLC
Chambersburg PA
CBHW050447110726

47899CB00003B/836